D0552927

The Childminder's Companion

More related titles

Book-keeping and Accounting for the Small Business
How to keep the books and maintain financial control over your business

'. . . compulsory reading for those starting a new business and for those already in the early stages.' Manager, National Westminster Bank (Midlands)

Preparing a Winning Business Plan
How to win the attention of investors and stakeholders

'This book will not only help you prepare a business plan but will also provide a basic understanding of how to start up a business.' *Working from Home*

The Small Business Start-up Workbook
A step-by-step book to starting the business you've dreamed of

'A comprehensive and very practical workbook offering a modern approach to self-employment. . . A *must have* for anyone thinking of setting up their own venture.' *Thames Valley News*

Work for Yourself and Reap the Rewards
How to master your destiny and be your own boss
'This book is written in a clear, concise and readable format. It's also very enjoyable.' CEO Business Enterprise Agency of South East Essex Ltd

howtobooks

Please send for a free copy of the latest catalogue:

How To Books
Spring Hill House, Spring Hill Road,
Begbroke, Oxford OX5 1RX, United Kingdom
info@howtobooks.co.uk
www.howtobooks.co.uk

The Childminder's Companion

A practical guide to looking after other people's children

Allison Lee

howtobooks

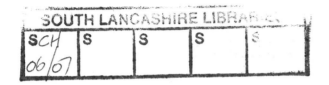

SOUTH LANCASHIRE LIBRARIES

SCH 06/07	S	S	S	S

LANCASHIRE COUNTY LIBRARY	
10625468	
Askews	

Published by How To Books Ltd
Spring Hill House, Spring Hill Road
Begbroke, Oxford OX5 1RX, United Kingdom
Tel: (01865) 375794 Fax: (01865) 379162
info@howtobooks.co.uk
www.howtobooks.co.uk

All rights reserved. No part of this work may be reproduced or stored in an information retrieval system (other than for purposes of review) without the express permission of the publisher in writing.

The right of Allison Lee to be identified as author of this work has been asserted by her in accordance with the Copyright, Designs and Patents Act 1988.

© Copyright 2007 Allison Lee

British Library Cataloguing in Publication Data.
A catalogue record for this book is available from the British Library.

ISBN: 978 1 84528 171 7

Cover design by Baseline Arts Ltd, Oxford
Produced for How To Books by Deer Park Productions, Tavistock
Typeset by PDQ Typesetting, Newcastle-under-Lyme, Staffs.
Printed and bound by Cromwell Press Ltd, Trowbridge, Wiltshire

NOTE: The material contained in this book is set out in good faith for general guidance and no liability can be accepted for loss or expense incurred as a result of relying in particular circumstances on statements made in the book. Laws and regulations are complex and liable to change, and readers should check the current position with the relevant authorities before making personal arrangements.

Contents

Acknowledgements

I would like to thank Nikki Read and Giles Lewis of How to Books for allowing me the opportunity of having this second book about childminding published through them. I am passionate about quality childcare and I strongly believe that every child has the right to feel loved and welcome in a happy, secure environment where they can explore and learn. I have endeavoured to provide such an environment for the many children I have worked with over the years I have spent as a childminder. This book has been written in the hope of sharing some of my ideas and experiences with other like-minded people who are either already working with children or who are considering moving into a profession involving working with children be it as a professional childminder, nursery nurse, early years worker or similar.

I would like to thank all the parents and the children, past and present, I have had the privilege of working with.

I would also like to thank my own parents, Roger and Cynthia, for providing me with a memorable childhood which has set me in good stead for being a mother and childcarer.

Last but by no means least I would like to thank my husband Mark and sons Sam and David for their patience and understanding which have enabled me to pursue such a demanding career.

Introduction

This book is intended as a follow up to my first book *Starting Your Own Childminding Business* and it will provide an essential guide for all childcare practitioners working in a home-based setting.

There are many different aspects to a childminder's duties and this book will help you to look closely at some of the more challenging areas of childcare. It should provide you with the help needed to make your business work effectively.

Children who are suitably entertained and stimulated by activities and resources, appropriate to their age and stage of development, are usually happy and content. Boredom is one of the main factors which results in disruptive or unwanted behaviour and it is important for childcare practitioners to recognise the needs of children of differing ages, and provide for their individual stages of development. In order to do this you will need to know how a child grows and develops and this book takes you through the stages of child development from birth to school age.

My own two boys, Sam and David, have given me the inspiration to work with children and, although now teenagers themselves, I treasure the fun years we had together when they were very young and enjoying discovering things for the first time. Childhood is a very special time and every child should have the opportunity to enjoy their early years. Many children today spend time with childminders or in a nursery and it is our duty, as childcare practitioners, to provide them with the opportunities they need to grow and develop into confident individuals.

Over the many years I have worked as a childminder I have come to realise the importance of keeping abreast of the job and, wherever necessary, I have tried to anticipate the areas of improvement within my business and rectify them before any problems have had the chance to arise. Like most jobs there will always be areas for concern but, with the help of this book, you should be able to recognise and correct these successfully.

1

Keeping Parents Happy

To make a success of any business it is important that you keep your customers happy and childminding is no exception. In addition to providing good quality childcare it is essential that you listen to what the parents and children are telling you, and that you make every effort to accommodate their wishes whenever possible.

ACKNOWLEDGING THE DIFFERENCES IN PARENTING STYLES

When you are caring for children from several families you should ensure that everyone is aware of the rules and policies of your setting. However it is vital that you also bear in mind that not everyone will have the same values or share the same views as yourself, and there may be times when compromises will have to be made by everyone.

There is no right or wrong way to bring up a child and it is probably true to say that parenting skills, rather than actually being learned, are usually passed on from our own parents. Parents have lived through thousands of years of rearing children and how we have been brought up ourselves, and the values we have had instilled in us by our own mothers and fathers, will have a huge affect on the way we in turn act as parents. Consequently what may work effectively in one family set-up may be totally unacceptable in another.

Working on the theory that our own parenting styles are heavily influenced by the way we have been brought up ourselves as children, it is probably true to say that today's parents are using skills which echo the styles of their parents before them. There are of course exceptions to every rule and an adult who feels they have been unfairly treated as a child, perhaps they felt their parents were too restricting or authoritarian, may well choose to bring their own offspring up in a more relaxed style.

Usually, however, parents want the best for their children. How they actually go about achieving this may vary immensely. The important thing to remember is that there are many different ways of successfully bringing up children and many different factors influencing the way parents choose to do this.

Factors which influence parenting styles

Some of the more common factors which can influence the way in which parents may choose to bring up their children include:

◆ money and employment;
◆ housing;
◆ education;
◆ family structure;
◆ culture;
◆ religion.

Generally speaking parenting styles fall into three main categories:

◆ authoritarian;
◆ permissive;
◆ authoritative.

Let us now look at these styles in more detail:

1. Authoritarian

This type of parenting tends to be controlling. These parents have many rules in an attempt to manage the behaviour of their children. Quite often authoritarian parents have very high expectations of their children which can often be difficult for the child to achieve.

2. Permissive

This tends to be the opposite of authoritarian. Permissive parents allow their children the freedom of choice. Often children with permissive parents are more difficult to manage when it comes to behaviour because they have been allowed much more freedom than other children. Although choice and responsibility are good for children, it is also essential that they are not allowed an excessive amount of freedom and it should be remembered that boundaries are essential in order for children to feel safe and secure.

3. Authoritative

This is the category which most parents fall into. Authoritative parents attempt to manage and control their child's behaviour in a way which enables them to be accepted into society. They take the time to listen to their children and to explain rules and expectations.

Family structures also have an enormous affect on parenting styles and the main structures are:

- the nuclear family;
- the extended family;
- the single parent family;
- the homosexual or lesbian family;
- the reconstituted family;
- the adoptive family.

Let us now look at these structures in more detail:

The nuclear family

This type of family structure consists of both parents and their children living together and sharing the responsibility of caring for their children.

The extended family

This type of family structure consists of parents, children and relatives all living close by and sometimes even in the same house and sharing the responsibility of bringing up the children. This kind of family structure was traditional in this country for centuries and is still common practice in many parts of the world.

The single parent family

This type of family structure consists of one parent living on their own with their children. This type of family occurs when the parents have divorced or separated, when one parent has died or when a woman has actively chosen to have a child without the support of the father.

The homosexual/lesbian family

This type of family structure consists of one natural parent living with a partner of the same sex, along with their children.

The reconstituted family

This type of family structure consists of one natural parent and one step parent living together with the children.

The adoptive family

This type of family structure consists of a child who is not living with one or both of their natural parents. Sometimes the child may be unaware that they are adopted and therefore appear to be part of a *nuclear* family structure.

TIP

Whatever type of family structure a child is brought up in, parents usually want the best for their children and, as there are no right or wrong ways to parenting, it is important to remain non-judgemental.

WHAT ARE PARENTS LOOKING FOR WITH REGARD TO CHILDCARE?

This question may at first appear to be an easy one to answer. However, on closer reflection it is more complex than originally thought. Different parents, and indeed their children, require different things from childcare. Influencing factors could well be the child's age and stage of development for instance. Generally speaking, parents are looking for childcare which offers their child the chance to be in a stimulating, safe environment. Additional factors they may be looking for are:

- ◆ a loving, caring environment;
- ◆ a chance to mix with other children;
- ◆ a chance to build on their confidence;
- ◆ a start to the child's education;
- ◆ a variety of experiences;
- ◆ an established routine which their child can relate to.

Safety

It is probably true to say that most parents looking for childcare are interested in the safety of the environment and the opportunities and experiences the childminder can offer their child. Ensuring safety is a very important part of a childminder's job and we will look at this in more detail in Chapter 3.

Benefits of choosing a childminder

Parents who chose a childminder over a nursery setting for their child will do so for a number of reasons. Although some nurseries offer excellent opportunities for children, childminders come into their own for several reasons:

- ◆ **Smaller groups**. Most childminders are registered to care for three children under the age of five years and can therefore offer a much more personal service.

- ◆ **The same carer**. Being cared for by the same person everyday has many benefits for a child and is preferable to having to get used to several carers in a nursery setting. This can be particularly beneficial to a child who finds new situations difficult to handle.

- ◆ **Continuity of care**. Childminders often care for children from several weeks old right through their school years. This is something that nurseries cannot offer and alternative childcare often has to be found once a child begins school.

- ◆ **Childminders often become an extension of the child's family** as excellent friendships are forged.

- **Childminders have a better knowledge and understanding** of the children as they are usually the only people, other than the child's parents, who are caring for the child and they are therefore in an excellent position to spot any changes in behaviour, for example, early on.

COMMON PROBLEMS AND HOW TO AVOID THEM

Contracts, policies and procedures

Today's working parents lead busy, stressful lives and, although it is true to say that most childminders also lead hectic lives and work long hours, this is often forgotten when a problem arises as people tend to see things only from their own point of view. When dealing with any type of complaint it is important to remember to:

- stay calm;
- listen to what the parents have to say;
- avoid interrupting when someone else is telling you something;
- get your own message across without resorting to apportioning blame;
- refrain from shouting or becoming aggressive.

Sometimes, even the most valued friendships and trusted relationships can experience problems and usually these occur through misunderstandings. It is absolutely paramount that childminders issue watertight contracts and foolproof policies and procedures and that they take the time to explain these to parents. Ideally all contracts, policies and procedures should be reviewed regularly, at least once a year. Displaying policies on the walls of your setting and referring to them often can eliminate problems and help to jog the memories of parents who may have mislaid their copy or simply forgotten its content.

Problems usually occur due to misunderstandings and this is where a watertight contract comes into its own. Always take the time to word your contracts accurately and explain their contents to parents before inviting them to sign. Make sure that they fully understand what is expected of them and what they in return can expect from you.

Your policies and procedures also go a long way to ensuring that misunderstandings do not occur and you should think carefully about what you are asking of parents and their children. Do not write policies which will be hard to achieve and avoid expecting too much from the children. Your policies and procedures should always be written with the age and comprehension level of the children in mind. Chapter 5 covers behaviour policies in more detail.

Dealing with common problems

Some of the more common problems which may arise are:

Behaviour

Often your own rules regarding behaviour may differ from those of the child's parents. However, it is important to remember that rules have to be made and kept, in order for all the children in your setting to be happy and enjoy their time with you. It must be made clear that you expect all the children to abide by your rules *regardless* of what they are allowed to do at home.

Payment

Problems can sometimes arise when parents become lax with their payments and fail to pay on time. These problems can easily be rectified by reminding parents of the contract you have with them and, if necessary, incorporating an additional fee into the contract for late payment. You will find that parents are unhappy paying extra and will ensure that they pay on time once you have exercised your rights to a late payment fee.

Dietary requirements

Ideally these issues will be discussed and agreed early on, before the child takes up a place with you. You must always seek the preference of parents where sweets, sugary snacks and fizzy drinks are concerned. Ideally these should be kept to a minimum regardless of parental preference; but you must never give a child any of these if their parents have specifically requested you not to.

Holidays

Like payments, these should be discussed and agreed prior to signing the contract. Often parents who have been happy to accept that you will have five weeks holiday a year become less accepting of this if your holiday dates are different to theirs and they need to find alternative cover for the time you are away. This problem can be avoided by liaising with the parents about dates and, where possible, giving them lots of notice or planning your holidays together so that your dates coincide.

No matter how hard you work, how many hours you devote to your business or how dedicated you are to your job, there are very few childminders who will not, at some point in their careers, come across a problem or receive a complaint. This is because all families are unique and will not agree with everything you do and say all of the time. As the saying goes you 'cannot please all of the people all of the time', however you should be striving to 'please most of the people most of the time'. If you take the time to listen to parents and accept that everyone is different, and that they have different opinions and values, then you will be well on the way to dealing with any potential problems should they arise.

DEALING WITH COMPLAINTS

If you are unfortunate enough to receive a complaint try to resolve the problem as amicably as possible. This is necessary both from a business point of view and from the child's point of view. Children can very quickly detect any animosity between their parents and their childminder and they will become upset and confused if their main carers are at loggerheads.

Encourage parents to meet with you, after work hours when interruptions are at a minimum, to discuss the problem. Allow them to put their point of view across, listen to them without interrupting and take on board what they are saying. After they have had their say, put your own point of view across in a calm and reasonable manner. Do not blame anyone, accept that there has been a difference of opinion and seek to resolve the matter.

Communicating with parents

When you are communicating with parents it is essential that you treat them as equals. Although it is important to get your own message across, it is equally important to listen to, value and respect the views of the parents, in order to establish a friendly relationship based on trust and mutual understanding. A poor relationship with the child's parents will inevitably cause problems in the long run.

When communicating with parents it is important to remember that this may not necessarily be through the spoken word. Other forms of communication involve:

- body language;
- written language;
- tone of voice;
- touch;
- gestures;
- eye contact.

There may be times when other methods of communication may be necessary such as the use of pictures and symbols. A person who has a hearing impairment or who does not share the same language, for example, may need to communicate in this way. When communicating with parents it is important to remember to:

- **Show an interest** in the person who is speaking. Do not allow your gaze or thoughts to wander but focus on what the person is saying.

- **Really *listen*** to what you are being told.

- **Do not interrupt the speaker**. It is difficult for anyone to get their point across if they are constantly being interrupted.

- **Do not rush the speaker** – allow them the time to say what they wish to say at their own speed; do not finish their sentences for them or put words into their mouth.

By following the simple steps above you will become an effective listener. For a parent to be happy to speak to you about a potential problem, they have to be confident that what they tell you will be taken seriously and acted upon.

Body language says a lot about a person without them actually having to utter a word. It is important to be aware of what your *body* is saying as well as your *mouth*. If you are discussing a child's behaviour for example with their parent, and you are frowning and folding your arms across your chest, whilst narrating an incident of inappropriate behaviour, you will appear defensive. Likewise, by standing with your hands on your hips you will give the message that you are expecting aggression.

Body language can be interpreted in many ways but the following table shows the most common possible interpretations.

Body language	Possible interpretation
Hands in pockets, shoulders hunched	Dejection
Head resting in hands	Boredom
Head tilted to one side	Interest
Biting nails	Nervous
Fiddling with hair	Insecure
Stroking the chin	Making a decision
Rubbing hands together	Anticipation
Hands clasped behind the back	Angry, frustrated
Crossed legs, foot swinging	Boredom
Brisk walk	Confident

TIP

The most important thing to remember when communicating with parents is to treat them as equals. Whatever their family structure or values you must listen to them and respect their wishes. Parents are *the* most important people in a child's life and must be treated accordingly.

2

Keeping Children Happy

Unlike parents, children are relatively easy to keep happy! They will not make any unreasonable demands on you and will not expect you to perform miracles. Children are usually happy and content if they feel safe, valued and are offered appropriate activities to stimulate their minds. It is of course your duty as a childminder to enhance this and encourage them to achieve to their full potential – and to ensure that they are loved, welcomed and valued.

In order for Ofsted to make their judgement about the overall quality of your childminding setting the inspector will ask the very important question: *What is it like for a child here?* The inspector will judge how well you meet a series of outcomes for children that are set out in the Children Act 2004. These outcomes are as follows:

- How do you help children to be healthy?

- How do you protect children from harm or neglect and help them to stay safe?

- How do you help children to enjoy themselves and achieve their full potential?

- How do you help children to make a positive contribution to your setting and to the wider community?

CHILDREN'S RIGHTS

The United Nations Convention on the Rights of the Child is an international treaty which applies to everyone under the age of 18 years and consists of 54 agreed articles. There are certain Acts of Parliament which are in place to promote the equality of opportunity and to prevent discrimination. The Acts include the Children Act 1989 which requires that the regulatory body has a set of policies in practice for equality of opportunity and that these policies are reviewed regularly. All childcare practitioners should receive regular updates relating to equal opportunities and they should be provided with details of any relevant training as and when necessary.

The Children Act 1989 acknowledges the importance of the child's wishes and opinions. The Act emphasises the need for parents and carers to be *responsible* for their children rather than to have *rights over* them.

It is because children cannot always stand up for themselves and be heard that this set of rights has been made and they take into account a child's vulnerability. Almost every country in the world has agreed to and signed the United Nations Convention underlining its importance.

PROVIDING FOR CHILDREN'S NEEDS

Children have five basic needs. These needs are illustrated in Figure 1.

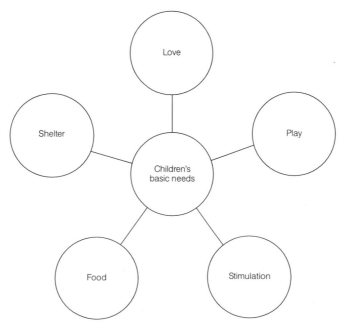

Fig. 1. Children's five basic needs.

The basic human rights of children entitle them to things such as food, health care and protection from abuse. However a child's rights are different from those of an adult as children cannot always stand up for themselves. Children need a special set of rights which take into account their vulnerability and which ensure that adults take responsibility for their protection, stimulation and development. The UN Convention on the Rights of the Child outlines the basic human rights of *all* children *everywhere*.

All children have the right to:

◆ survival;
◆ protection from harm, abuse and exploitation;
◆ develop to their full potential;
◆ participate fully in social, cultural and family life;
◆ express their views;
◆ have their views listened to, valued and taken into account;
◆ play, rest and enjoy their lives.

There are certain rights outlined in the UN Convention which relate particularly to childcare and education and it is these rights of the child that childminders should be most concerned with. The rights which affect childcare are as follows:

◆ Children have the right to sufficient food and clean water for their needs.
◆ Children have the right to appropriate health care and medicines.
◆ Children have the right to be with their family or those who will care for them best.
◆ Children have the right to play.
◆ Children have the right to be safe and free from harm and neglect.
◆ Children have the right to free education.
◆ Children should not be exploited as cheap labour or soldiers.
◆ Children have the right to an adequate standard of living.
◆ Disabled children have the right to special care and training.

MISSING MUMMY OR DADDY?

It is probably true to say that the most difficult time for a childminder to keep a child happy is when the child is new to the setting and is missing their parents. This is particularly true for a young child who has been with their mother from birth and who may now need a childminder in order for their mother to return to work. You will not be able to take the place of the child's mother whilst they are in your setting, and you should not be striving to do this. It is your job to reassure the child, offer appropriate activities and comfort them when they are upset.

You will have to adjust your usual routine to cater for the new child and to offer additional support until they have settled into your setting.

In some ways it is easier to settle a young baby into your setting than an older child. However babies, when they get to the age of around eight months, start to become aware of strangers and may well go through a phase of missing mummy. Babies of this age can often become upset when being left and you would be wise to prepare the parents for this possibility.

Likewise the parents of the child may be very likely to miss their baby and may also need your support and reassurance.

SETTLING IN

Ideally before a child starts their placement with you, you will have had the opportunity to meet them on several occasions. You may decide to arrange to visit them in their own home and to get to know them on 'familiar territory' or you may prefer to arrange short visits at your own house so that the child can get used to their new setting; you may even decide on a mixture of both. It is important to discuss with the parents which strategy they feel will work best for their child.

Prior to a baby or child starting in your care you will need to gather from their parents as much information about them as possible in order to prepare yourself for the task ahead. The more information you have about a child – their likes, dislikes, fears and anxieties – the more equipped you will be to deal with any scenarios thrown at you.

It is important to remember that parents may feel equally, if not more, anxious than their child. They may have feelings of guilt about leaving their child. Reassure them that these feelings are all perfectly normal and offer them the support they need.

Tips for settling children into your childminding setting

♦ Arrange short visits prior to the placement commencing, in order to allow the child time to get to know their surroundings.

♦ Encourage parents to stay with their child for a while, particularly during the first few days, if this is possible.

♦ Offer support and encouragement to both the child and their parents.

♦ Encourage the child to bring a special toy or comforter from home.

♦ Avoid forcing the child to join in activities or games. If they prefer to sit and watch for a while, allow them to do this and to mix only when they are ready.

♦ Offer cuddles and reassurance if the child becomes distressed; remember to allow the child to take the lead on this level and never force a child to sit with you and be cuddled if they do not want to do so.

♦ Offer simple, straightforward activities immediately after their parent has left to take their mind off the separation. Ideally you will have discovered what particular activities the child prefers and will be able to offer these. Avoid anything which requires a lot of concentration.

Saying goodbye

Once a parent has decided they are going, encourage them to do just that! Long, drawn-out goodbyes are not a good idea, and can be stressful for everyone. Encourage the parents to establish a routine for saying goodbye and to stick to it. Children may become very upset if the departure is delayed and a child who is not crying at the start of the farewell may well be hysterical by the time it has finished! Always encourage the parent to actually say goodbye and kiss the child. *Never* allow them to sneak off without telling their child they are going. This may result in the child becoming clingy as they will come to expect their parent to disappear. If a child does not understand where their parent has gone they may suffer unnecessary distress and become distrustful.

TIP

Encourage parents to follow the 'SAS' rule when saying goodbye to their children: 'Short and Simple!'

Below is a routine which you may like to encourage parents to follow when saying goodbye to their child, particularly in the early stages of the placement when the child is still settling into your setting.

◆ Parent and child arrive at your house.
◆ Greet both the parent and child warmly as they come in.
◆ Either you or the parent takes the child's coat off.
◆ Ideally, in the case of an older child, you will already have a suitable activity prepared and you should then tell them about it.
◆ Prior to the child commencing the activity, encourage them to kiss their parent and say goodbye.
◆ Encourage the parent to tell their child that they are going and that they will be back at lunchtime/teatime etc.
◆ Allow the parent and child to say goodbye in their own way.
◆ Parent leaves.

Obviously the above routine will differ if the child is a young baby but, as with an older child, encourage the parents to say goodbye and allow the baby to see them leave rather than them sneaking off.

3

Safety in the Childcare Setting

THE IMPORTANCE OF SAFETY

As I have previously mentioned, safety is one of the factors embodied by the UN Convention. All children have the right to *be kept safe* and it is your duty as a childminder to ensure that the children in your care are not exposed to any unnecessary dangers whilst in your setting. Deciding on safety measures in your home is not always easy and it is not simply a case of eliminating potential problems such as placing guards around fires, which in the main are common sense measures. You also need to anticipate a child's moves and see things from *their* perspective. When caring for children you need to be on your guard at all times and be aware of any potential hazards which may pose a threat in your particular setting.

Standard 6 of the English National Standards, to which all childminders in England must conform, states 'the registered person takes positive steps to promote safety within the setting and on outings and ensures proper precautions are taken to prevent accidents'.

I cannot stress enough that you can never have too many safety measures in place. True, children need to explore their environment and, to a certain extent, they need to discover and learn things for themselves. However it is not acceptable for a child to suffer serious injury whilst they are doing so. You have a responsibility to protect the children in your care and you must do this to the very best of your ability. It is not acceptable to be lax when it comes to safety and although accidents can take only seconds to occur the consequences of them can last a lifetime. There is a fine line between allowing a child freedom to explore and protecting them from injury, and you must make a professional judgement as to just how much a child should be expected to know.

Young children have no understanding of danger and do not think about the consequences their actions may have. This is why you have to think for them. Supervision is paramount. Adequate supervision should be given to children *at all* times and this is probably the most important safety procedure you can follow. Without adequate supervision all the safety measures in the world will not prevent a child from harming themselves.

ESSENTIAL GUIDE FOR PROMOTING SAFETY IN THE HOME

Safety needs to be considered in a variety of ways including:

1. Safety in the home.
2. Equipment safety.
3. Safety in the garden.
4. Safety on trips and outings.
5. Safety in the car.
6. Safety around animals and pets.
7. Safety at mealtimes.
8. Food hygiene.
9. Personal hygiene.
10. Stranger danger.

In addition to the above issues you also need to be aware of how to prevent accidents. We will look closely at each of these points next.

1. Safety in the home

Children love to explore, of this there is little doubt. Things which may seem of little consequence to us such as a trailing flex, a bookshelf or a potted house plant, pose potential hazards to a young child. However it is impossible to eliminate every single item which may pose a danger to children bar encompassing them in a padded cell empty of any toys or equipment, and you should not be striving to 'wrap them up in cotton wool'. What you should be trying to achieve is a safe environment, as free from potential dangers as possible where the child can play and learn in a well supervised, safe environment.

In order to achieve this inside the home you need to assess the areas which you use when caring for children and look at all the potential dangers carefully, eliminating each one where possible. Every room in the house will pose some kind of a threat to young children and it is best to look at each room separately to ascertain which hazards need to be addressed.

Lounge, dining room, sitting room and playroom

These are the areas where children will probably be spending most of their time and as such you should be extra vigilant when assessing for potential hazards. It may be a good idea to get down on your hands and knees and see your setting from a young child's view point. Trailing flexes are easy to miss from an adult's height but, once you drop to your knees, you will instantly see the dangers these flexes can pose if they wrap around a child's neck or trip them up if their legs become entangled in them. Other potential hazards you should look out for include:

♦ **Heating appliances**. Fires should be fitted with an appropriate guard and radiators should not be allowed to get so hot that they burn if touched. If necessary radiator covers should be fitted.

♦ **Glass**. If your living areas have glass doors or windows which are low then these must be fitted with safety or laminated glass. Safety or glass film must be fitted to glass cabinets, coffee tables etc if these are accessible to children.

♦ **Electric sockets**. When not in use all electric sockets which are within a child's reach should be fitted with socket covers.

♦ **Blinds**. Ensure that any cords are kept well out of the reach of children who have been known to become entangled in them and strangled.

- **Televisions, DVDs and video recorders**. All electrical appliances should be safe from prying fingers and, ideally, guards should be fitted to prevent children from posting toys and other objects into video slots.

- **Rugs and mats**. Make sure that these are not frayed and cannot be tripped over.

- **House plants**. Keep plants out of the reach of children and avoid any poisonous varieties particularly at Christmas time when people are tempted to purchase mistletoe and holly.

- **Table cloths**. Always make sure that these do not dangle over the edge of the table enabling a child to pull the contents on top of them.

- **Ornaments**. Avoid placing ornaments within reach of children and never place objects on low window ledges. Small trinkets should be placed well out of the reach of children.

- **Toys**. Make sure that toys and play equipment are in a good, clean state of repair. Toys with missing or broken parts should be either repaired or replaced. Always look for appropriate safety labels and make sure children do not play with toys that are not suitable for their age, particularly if they contain small parts which may pose a choking hazard.

Kitchen

Kitchens are especially hazardous to children and they should not be allowed to play in the kitchen at any time. Children should always be supervised by an adult when in the kitchen. Pay particular attention to:

- **Cookers**. Make sure that children are not at risk of burning from hot oven doors and that they cannot reach pans on the hob. Always turn pan handles inwards.

- **Glass cabinets**. Safety or laminated glass must be used or safety film fitted to all glass door cabinets.

- **Electrical sockets**. If not in use, sockets should be fitted with appropriate covers.

- **Fridges and freezers**. Locks should be fitted to prevent access to children.

- **Knives**. Always store knives out of the reach and sight of children, preferably in a locked cupboard.

- **Kettles**. Always ensure that kettles are pushed to the back of the work surface and that no flexes are trailing down.

- **Toasters**. Again these should be pushed toward the back of the work surface and all flexes stored out of children's reach.

- **Drawers and cupboards**. These should be fitted with locks where necessary and dangerous items such as knives, scissors, string, plastic bags, medicines and cleaning materials should be stored in cupboards high up and out of the reach of children.

- **Dishwashers**. Always make sure that these are closed and, when stacking them, place knives and other sharp objects point down to avoid a child falling onto them. Ideally children should not be around when you are loading and unloading the dishwasher.

- **Washing machines and tumble driers**. Keep the doors to these appliances firmly closed at all times and, where possible fit, *and use*, safety locks.

If necessary, consider investing in a safety gate or child proof barrier in order to prevent children from accessing the kitchen area without your knowledge.

Halls, stairs and landings

These areas may be particularly appealing to children as they can climb on banisters, jump down stairs, and so on. What may seem like a good way of playing to a child, may in fact be potentially dangerous. Consider aspects such as:

- **Stair gates**. These should always be used at both the top and the bottom of a flight of stairs. Ideally you should fit a type of gate which opens rather than one which requires you to 'step over' it as these pose potential dangers for tripping and falling particularly if installed at the top of a flight of stairs.

- ◆ **Smoke detectors**. These should be fitted on every level and the batteries should be checked regularly and replaced when necessary.

- ◆ **Carpets**. These should fit securely and should not be worn or frayed.

- ◆ **Glass doors and windows**. Use safety or laminated glass or apply safety film.

- ◆ **Banisters**. These should conform to the national standards and it should not be possible for children to get their heads through the gaps in the rails. Never allow children to play on or swing from the banisters and ensure that they are not allowed to climb up onto hand rails.

- ◆ **Lighting**. Use adequate lighting at all times.

Bedrooms

Pay particular attention to the following safety aspects in the bedrooms:

- ◆ **Glass windows and doors**. Safety or laminated glass should be fitted or safety film used.

- ◆ **Electrical sockets**. When not in use these should be fitted with appropriate covers.

- ◆ **Cupboards and drawers**. Always ensure that medicines, toiletries and cosmetics are stored out of the sight and reach of children.

TIP

Children are naturally curious and they will taste and chew things left around them. It can of course be very dangerous for a child to swallow medicines or household chemicals and cleaning products and they must be kept out of the sight and reach of children at all times, preferably in a locked cupboard. Remember that although these products often have child-resistant tops, they can never be 100% child proof.

Bathrooms

Bathrooms can be very dangerous places for children and, although children should not be allowed to play in bathrooms you should use your judgement with regard to supervision in this room, bearing in mind the child's age and their need for privacy.

- **Water**. The temperature of the water should be set appropriately so as not to scald children when they wash their hands.

- **Medicine and bathroom cabinets**. Medicines should be stored out of children's reach and cabinets fitted with suitable locks.

- **Toilet seats/steps**. Toilet seats, which fit over the usual adult seat to enable young children to sit comfortably on the toilet, need to fit securely and be free from cracks or splits. Provide a suitable step to enable the child to reach the toilet safely without having to climb.

- **Changing mats**. These should be clean and free from splits or tears.

Hygiene in the bathroom must be excellent and you will need to ensure that this area is kept scrupulously clean, particularly if a number of young children are using the facilities every day. Remember to clean the whole of the toilet, around the rim and the handle in addition to the seat.

Of course safety measures are not simply restricted to the rooms in our homes. We must also ensure that the equipment we use and the toys we provide are safe and free from potential hazards.

TIP

Think about how the children in your care are kept safely *within* the house. Consider securing a safety chain to the outside doors to prevent active toddlers from venturing outside without your knowledge.

2. Equipment safety

- **Highchairs**. These must be clean and in a good state of repair. Always wipe down highchairs after each use with a suitable disinfectant solution to remove any traces of food particles. Check highchairs regularly for loose or worn parts and *always* use correctly fitted reins to strap the child securely into the highchair.

◆ **Pushchairs**. These must be in a good state of repair. Check regularly for loose or worn parts and, again, correctly fitted reins must *always* be used.

TIP

Reins are inexpensive to purchase. Consider buying two sets and leave one permanently on the highchair and one in the pushchair so that you don't have to continually swap them over or risk forgetting to use them.

◆ **Car seats**. These must be adjusted and fitted into the car correctly to be effective. *Never* leave a child sat in a car seat on top of a table or chair. Always place them on the floor, away from hazards.

◆ **Potties/toilet seats**. These must be kept scrupulously clean and free from cracks and splits. After use, the contents of potties should be flushed down the toilet and a suitable disinfectant solution used to clean them. *Never* empty urine down the sink.

◆ **Changing mats**. These must be kept scrupulously clean and free from splits and tears which could harbour germs and bacteria. Mats should be wiped down with a disinfectant solution after each use.

◆ **Baby walkers**. These can be very dangerous as babies can easily overbalance them. Evidence suggests that baby walkers, far from encouraging children to walk, may actually hinder their development and childminders are advised not to use this item of equipment.

◆ **Beds and cots**. Children can fall out of beds and cots and it is for this reason that they should be seen as potential areas for accidents. Check that cots with sides which slide down are securely fastened to avoid being undone by young children. Consider using rails fitted to the side of beds to avoid children from falling out, however bear in mind that some children see these rails as potential climbing frames! Top bunks should never be used for young children.

Ensure that all mattresses fit the cots and beds snugly to prevent children from slipping down between them and the bars or frames. Pillows should never be used for children under the age of 18 months.

◆ **Fire equipment**. All childminders must ensure that smoke detectors, fire extinguishers and fire blankets are fitted in their homes and that these are checked regularly. Fire extinguishers and blankets should be placed in prominent places and you should be confident using them. Test smoke alarms regularly and replace batteries when necessary.

3. Safety in the garden

Outside areas can be very hazardous for children and it is your duty as a childminder to eliminate as many of these potential hazards as possible. Think carefully about the outside space that you have and plan carefully the best way to utilise this space. If your garden is large enough, you may like to fence off a specific area which can be designated specifically for the children you care for. If you are fortunate enough to have this option you should be able to create a well planned area which is completely child friendly.

If you are starting from scratch think about safety measures such as:

◆ Using bark around swings, climbing frames and slides to cushion any tumbles and falls the children may experience.

◆ Planting fragrant, visual plants and flowers which could form a 'sensory' garden for any child with impairments. You will be able to source plants, trees and shrubs which are safe for children and avoid the common poisonous plants such as daffodil bulbs, hyacinths and ivy which most gardens tend to have!

◆ Appropriate fencing to ensure that children are kept securely when playing outdoors and cannot access roads, greenhouses, water butts, drains or other hazards.

◆ Creating a large covered area for sand. Children love to build and experiment with sand and sand pits are very appealing. Unfortunately they are not simply appealing to children; every cat in the neighbourhood will use it as a toilet if not covered securely!

It does not have to be very expensive to create a special child friendly outdoor area nor does the area have to very large. Providing the children are safe and can take part in outdoor activities you can let your imagination run wild.

Don't despair if you are not fortunate to have the space to create a separate area for the children and you find yourself having to make the most of what you have and adapting it to provide a suitable, safe 'playground'. The most important thing you must do is ensure that the children cannot access:

- ponds or water features;
- greenhouses;
- water butts;
- compost heaps;
- dustbins;
- drains;
- hazardous plants;
- garden sheds;
- garden tools or machinery;
- clothes lines;
- roads.

4. Safety on trips and outings

Ensuring that children are safe is not only a necessity whilst you are on your own childminding premises. It is your responsibility, as a childminder, to make certain that the children in your care are safe and free from harm *at all times*, and this includes while you are taking or collecting them from playgroup, nursery or school, visiting the playground, shops or library, enjoying a day in the park or simply going for a walk. All of these trips and outings pose potential threats to young children and you must think carefully about the ages and stages of development of the children in your care and make suitable arrangements for their safety. Consider the following recommendations:

- Use reins or wrist straps for young children to prevent them from running off or getting lost. They are particularly useful if you are on a busy road or in a crowded place.

- Teach older children the 'Green Cross Code' and make sure they use it.

- Talk about road safety to younger children and show them how to cross roads safely, that is to stop, look and listen and never to cross between parked cars.

- Always take a mobile telephone and contact details of the children with you so that you can contact parents in the unfortunate event of an accident.

- Apply sun cream and hats in hot weather and ensure that babies and children are appropriately covered in ordered to prevent sunburn.

- Consider taking a travel first aid kit with you when out and about to use in the case of minor accidents.

- On hot days always take an adequate supply of water.

When out walking make sure you use zebra or pelican crossings to cross roads whenever possible and, when walking alongside roads, ensure that children walk on the inside, away from the traffic. On narrow paths when it is not possible to walk side by side, children should walk *in front* of you so that you can see them at all times and you should walk *facing* the oncoming traffic.

TIP

Children, below the age of about 12 years, cannot judge distance and should not be allowed to cross roads unassisted. Teach children about road safety but bear in mind that they may not always remember what they have been taught and may need constant reminders!

5. Safety in the car

- Always ensure that you have insurance to cover the use of your car as part of your childminding business when transporting children.

◆ When travelling by car, always put children in or take them out of the car on the kerb side of the road to keep them away from other vehicles.

◆ Always use appropriate child seats and ensure that these are fitted in the car correctly. Make sure each child has their own seat and that they are securely fastened in it.

◆ Passengers should *never* exceed the number of seats available in the car and children should not be allowed to travel on an adult's knee.

◆ Never leave children alone and unsupervised in a car, not even for short periods of time.

◆ Always turn off the engine whilst you are packing or unpacking the vehicle.

◆ Never leave children unattended on the pavement whilst you are packing the car with shopping or putting the pushchair into the boot. Always strap the children in the car first and then load the car so that you can be sure that they are safe and not tempted to wander off.

◆ Use child safety locks to ensure that doors can only be opened from the outside to prevent children from opening them whilst the car is in motion.

◆ Never buy a second-hand car seat as it may:
   a) not conform to the latest safety standards;
   b) have suffered damage in a previous accident which you cannot see;
   c) not come with fitting instructions. It is vital that car seats are fitted correctly in order to be effective;
   d) have parts missing.

6. Safety around animals and pets

Although it is important not to unduly frighten or worry children around animals and pets you should always make sure that they are aware of the potential dangers they may pose. Quite often adults can unwittingly pass their own fears of certain animals onto their children. I have witnessed several occasions when a parent who is afraid of horses or dogs has unintentionally conditioned their children to have the same fear. They may do this by avoiding the animal they themselves are afraid of or by telling their child frightening stories of their own experiences. This is not advisable. Whenever possible avoid using scare tactics in order to teach children caution; instead teach children how to act sensibly around animals and pets and to take care not to startle or hurt them.

Some children may well have pets of their own at home and feel no fear whatsoever towards dogs the size of a small donkey, whilst others may be fearful of even the smallest of breeds. Always make sure you are sensitive to each individual child's feelings and *never* force a child to stroke a dog if they are not happy to do so. Ridiculing a child or making them feel inadequate because of their fear is not acceptable. Forcing a child to befriend an animal they are not entirely comfortable around may cause them undue stress and add to their fears.

It is always advisable to warn children of the potential dangers that pets and animals pose, but do so in words appropriate to their age and understanding. A child who loves dogs and perhaps even has a pet dog will probably happily stroke one she meets whilst out and about. However, much as the dog may be friendly this may not always be the case and the child needs to understand that it is not a good idea to stroke *any* dog they meet but perhaps only those they know well so that you can both be sure that the dog is not going to growl or bite.

Horses can also be attractive to young children who will invariably want to stroke and feed them. If you are going to allow the children to feed them make sure you are familiar with the horses yourself and that they are happy around young children and will not bite. Show the children how to hold the apple, carrot or grass: on the palm of a *flat* hand to avoid unintentional chewing of the fingers!

TIP

Remember that some horses are not used to young children and could easily be unnerved by nimble feet running around them. Don't allow the children to go up behind a horse or to scream and shout nearby.

There are of course many types of animals and pets that you and the children you care for may come into contact with at some point, but the most important things to remember are:

◆ If you own a pet dog or cat make sure that they are regularly wormed and treated for fleas and that they are up to date with any necessary inoculations.

◆ Never feed dogs at the table.

◆ Never allow children to play near feeding bowls.

◆ Teach your dog not to jump up.

◆ Do not allow young children to handle pets roughly.

◆ Remind children that pets are not toys and that it is possible to hurt them unintentionally.

◆ Always make sure that everyone who has handled pets, animals or their feeding bowls washes their hands thoroughly afterwards.

◆ Discourage children from kissing pets.

◆ Do not allow pets to lick faces.

7. Safety at mealtimes

Mealtime safety is not something that a lot of people give much consideration to in the same way as we think about other aspects of safety, but mealtimes can pose a threat to young children if they are not adequately supervised. You are probably already aware of the necessity to ensure that the food you serve to babies and very young children without teeth should be soft enough for them to swallow and digest. Yet, choking is not confined to babies and very small children. Children of any age can choke if they try to swallow something without chewing properly as it may become lodged in the throat and block the airway.

Grapes are particularly hazardous and there have been several cases reported of young children choking to death on grapes. Whole grapes should never be given to a small child; always cut the grapes in halves or quarters so that they do not become lodged in the throat. Peanuts are another particularly dangerous food to feed young children and you should never offer these as they can easily cause choking or, if inhaled into the lungs, can cause infection and lung damage.

Young children should be supervised closely at mealtimes. Be particularly vigilant when encouraging them to try finger foods as they will often cram food into their mouths rather than bite off a piece. Food such as bread and cake can then become dry and stodgy and difficult to chew so the child may try to swallow which can result in choking.

Checklist to avoid choking:

✓ Always supervise children at mealtimes.

✓ Be extra vigilant when children are trying finger foods such as banana, carrot, apple, etc.

✓ Offer small pieces of food rather than whole amounts as children are prone to cramming food into their mouths rather than biting a piece off.

✓ Never prop babies up with a feeding bottle – always hold them whilst they are feeding.

✓ Make sure that children are sat at a table when eating and drinking, and do not allow them to wander around with cups or cutlery.

8. Food hygiene

Food hygiene is a very important part of a childminder's daily routine. You not only need to know how to prepare and cook food safely but also how to store it. Good food hygiene is essential for the prevention of food poisoning. The very old and the very young are particularly vulnerable to the bacteria which causes food poisoning, also known as gastroenteritis. Anyone who has suffered from gastroenteritis will know that some of the symptoms suffered range from diarrhoea, vomiting, fever, headaches, stomach cramps and nausea. At best you could be laid up in bed for a few days, at worst, food poisoning can be fatal.

Bacteria thrive in moist, warm foods rich in protein such as:

◆ meat;
◆ poultry;
◆ milk;
◆ cream;
◆ seafood;
◆ prepared dishes containing egg;
◆ soups and gravy.

Bacteria thrives best at body temperature (37°C). It multiplies quickly, particularly in fresh foods, and cannot always be recognised as it may not cause the food to appear bad or to smell or taste unpleasant.

It is estimated that there are about *four times more* food poisoning incidents as a result of food prepared in the home than there are from food prepared on commercial premises such as restaurants and hotels. Every food business has a responsibility to make sure that the food they provide is fit for human consumption. As a childminder, if you provide food for the children you care for, *you are running a food business*. As such you are required to comply with the requirements of the Food Safety (General Food Hygiene) Regulations 1995 and certain parts of your home, i.e. food storage, preparation and cooking areas, will be eligible for inspection.

When storing food always:

◆ Keep food cold. Use a thermometer in your fridge to ensure that the temperature is always between 1-5°C). Be extra careful in the hot summer months or when the fridge is at its fullest. Avoid opening the fridge door often as this allows warm air to enter and alter the temperature of the interior.

◆ Make sure that food is cold *before* you place it in the fridge. Cooked food should be cooled quickly and then placed in the fridge.

◆ Store foods carefully to avoid cross-contamination. Raw food should be stored at the bottom of the fridge to prevent blood and juices from meat dripping onto other foodstuffs.

- Use cling film or other food wrap to cover food before placing it in the fridge.

- Make sure you clearly label and date food stored in the freezer and never be tempted to use foodstuffs which have passed their use by dates.

- Do not re-freeze anything which has been defrosted.

When preparing food always:

- Wash your hands before touching any foodstuff. Use warm soapy water and a clean towel.

- Never cough or sneeze near food or preparation areas.

- Make sure any cuts or other injuries are covered appropriately with a waterproof dressing.

- It is illegal for childminders to smoke whilst working with children. If you are preparing food for their consumption when they are not present, remember that it is still illegal to smoke in any room that is used for food preparation.

- Make sure you wear a clean apron.

- Make sure your kitchen is spotlessly clean, including work surfaces, utensils, cloths, floors, fridges, microwaves, toasters, grills, ovens, dishwashers, dustbins, etc.

- Do not allow pets near food preparation areas.

- Keep flies and other insects away – pay particular attention to this in the summer months. Use mesh or other suitable coverings over windows in food preparation areas.

- Keep waste bins covered and do not allow them to become over filled. Empty them regularly.

When cooking food always:

- Follow the instructions carefully and cook food thoroughly.

- Keep the oven spotlessly clean and wipe up spills immediately.

- Avoid eating leftovers – these are a particularly common cause of food poisoning.

- Avoid re-heating food.

TIP

Foods which are particularly prone to causing food poisoning and which require extra care when preparing and cooking include:

- chicken and other poultry;
- joints of meat;
- dishes containing mince such as beef burgers;
- dishes containing eggs.

Always make sure that these foods are cooked thoroughly.

---

9. Personal hygiene

Children should be taught good personal hygiene methods. One of the most important things you can do to encourage children to practise personal hygiene is to provide them with a good role model. Make sure you yourself follow good practice and set high standards for your own personal hygiene.

Children are more likely to develop infections than adults for several reasons:

- Their immune systems have not developed and will be immature.
- They may lack good personal hygiene standards.
- They need to be taught the necessity of frequently washing hands.

Although you should not be too worried about hygiene to the extent that you become obsessive, you do need to teach children about the importance of cleanliness and maintaining a personal hygiene routine. Teach children to:

◆ Wash their hands frequently especially after:
visiting the toilet;
handling pets;
coughing;
sneezing;
wiping noses.
Or before:
eating;
handling food.

◆ Teach children the importance of having their own hairbrush and toothbrush.

When following your own high personal hygiene standards make sure you take particular care when:

◆ Changing nappies or cleaning up other waste like vomit. Always wear protective gloves and an apron and dispose of the waste carefully in a sealed bag, before placing in an *outside* dustbin.

◆ Use a suitable disinfectant solution to wash down the infected area or changing mat.

10. Stranger danger

Whilst it is important to teach children the dangers of 'stranger danger', it is equally important to ensure that you do not unduly frighten them whilst doing so! Children do need to know the possible dangers they may come across and what to do if they are ever in a situation which they cannot handle. Firstly, it is important to help children to understand exactly what a stranger is.

Strangers may be:
✓ normal everyday people;
✓ both men and women;
✓ friendly and approachable.

Strangers may appear perfectly 'normal'. They are not necessarily dirty, weird or creepy, nor do they always act suspiciously. Although paedophiles are *usually* men, some women have been known to abuse children. Paedophiles do not fall into a particular 'category' and can come from all walks of life, professions and religious or racial backgrounds.

Strangers may:
✓   ask for advice or directions;
✓   offer lifts;
✓   offer sweets or money;
✓   ask for assistance in finding something they have 'lost' such as a dog/purse/keys, etc.

Paedophiles look for their victims by hanging around the kinds of places children are likely to be such as:

◆ schools;
◆ shopping centres;
◆ amusement arcades;
◆ theme parks;
◆ recreational parks;
◆ playgrounds;
◆ fun fairs;
◆ swimming baths.

Strangers to be wary of may be on foot or in a car. The important thing to teach children is *never* to go with someone they do not know no matter how genuine they appear to be or how plausible their request.

TIP

Discuss with the parents of the children you care for a suitable strategy for children to use in emergencies such as if they were approached by a stranger. Ask the parents to remind their children of stranger danger and to highlight the points you have already made so that you are working together and using the same tactics.

Checklist to help protect children from stranger danger:

◆ Teach children that they should never go off with anyone without telling the grown-up who is responsible for them. This includes people they know well and trust.

◆ Teach children to tell the adult who is responsible for them if they have been approached by a stranger and make sure that they realise that it is not their fault.

◆ Teach children that it is alright to kick, scream, shout and create loud noises if they feel threatened.

◆ Teach children what to do in the event that they may become separated from you or the adult they are with.

◆ When a child is old enough, teach them important facts such as their address and telephone number.

Children should be aware of who they can approach if they feel scared, threatened or if someone tries to entice them away. Make children aware that it is safe to approach:

◆ a police officer in uniform;
◆ a traffic warden;
◆ a security guard;
◆ a shop assistant;
◆ an adult who has other children with them.

If children get lost teach them to go into a shop or a place with lots of people. Tell them they must *never* go into a house, office, telephone booth, etc. with anyone. Make sure they are aware that they must *never* get into a car or accept a lift from anyone.

4

Factors Influencing Children's Behaviour

Before we can really begin to understand what makes a child behave in the way that they do we must first take a look at the factors which play an important part in their lives and which may actually influence their behaviour. Often, without us even realising it, the things around us and the aspects of our everyday lives, have a great influence on the way we conduct ourselves. Children are no exception. Whilst some appear resilient and take things in their stride, others are very sensitive and may have difficulty adjusting to changes.

One of the main factors which may affect a child's behaviour is their overall development. For example, a child may behave in a certain way because they have emotional difficulties or because their development is delayed. The way a child feels about themselves will also have an affect on their behaviour; it is very important that children are made to feel secure, loved and valued by the adults around them as these three factors create the basis of self-esteem and confidence.

Other factors which may influence the way a child acts and behaves include:

- divorce;
- separation;
- re-marriage;
- bereavement;
- birth of a new baby;
- moving house;
- starting/moving school;
- unemployment;

◆ race, culture and religion;
◆ child abuse.

The way a child copes with any of the above situations will depend primarily on the way they have been brought up, their own genetic makeup and their stage of development.

We will now look at these factors in more detail.

SEPARATION AND DIVORCE

Major changes, such as their parents' separation or divorce, can have a profound affect on a child's behaviour.

In today's society there are many pressures and problems facing parents. The divorce rate is especially high in the United Kingdom and often children of a very young age have to contend with the break up of their family life as they know it. We can never really be sure how divorce affects children but we can do our best to reassure them and prepare them for the changes ahead.

Exactly how much a child suffers may not really be known until much later in their lives when they begin to forge relationships and families of their own. Children may experience many feelings when their parents' relationship breaks down including:

◆ hurt;
◆ anger;
◆ resentment;
◆ sadness;
◆ guilt.

Over a quarter of the babies born in the UK today are likely to experience parental separation before they reach school leaving age, and divorce is one of the most common adverse life events experienced by children. When parents separate children may blame themselves for their parents' unhappiness and question where they fit into the new set-up. It is important to remember that divorce affects all members of a family and not just the actual marriage partners. How the parents themselves deal with their child's emotions will have a very important influence on the outcome of the whole situation. What is absolutely vital is that the parents:

♦ Explain the situation *honestly* to their children in a manner suitable to their child's age and understanding.

♦ Make sure the child is aware that the break down of the relationship is not their fault.

♦ Make sure that the child is aware that *both* parents still love the child deeply.

♦ Never ask the child to choose between parents.

♦ Avoid berating each other in front of the child.

♦ Avoid apportioning blame in front of the child.

♦ Never expect the child to take sides.

Children will react differently to divorce depending on their age and level of understanding of the situation. However their reactions can be summarised in the following ways:

1. Pre-school children

As very young children are unlikely to understand the full implications of divorce they will probably become sad and frightened when their parents separate. It is not uncommon for young children to become very clingy and demanding and to refuse to be left alone even for a few minutes. Problems at bedtimes may occur and they may show aggression towards other children or their siblings.

2. Primary school-aged children

As with very young children this age group will also experience sadness and grief, however they are more likely to also experience anger particularly towards the parent with whom they are living. Blame may be apportioned to this parent whilst the absent parent may appear to be idealised.

3. Pre-adolescent children

Children of this age group are often unable to talk about their feelings as they experience pain and embarrassment acutely. They may appear detached and seek distraction in play and other activities. It is not uncommon for a pre-adolescent child to strongly side with one parent and even refuse to see the other.

4. Adolescents

Children of this age group are often experiencing many mixed emotions and may withdraw from family life in the event of a divorce or separation. One concern for children of this age group is that they do not seek distraction in 'friends' who may have an undesirable influence upon them.

Security for children is paramount and this security comes from consistent love and discipline and from parents who are 'available' for their children. Security can be just as effective even if it comes from separate homes and divorced parents. Parents who work together can make dramatic changes easier to accept and manage and it is essential that both parents work together to find a solution which is suitable for *everyone*.

Below are some helpful tips for parents who are separating or divorcing and for their child's childminder to follow:

♦ Recognise the child's need to grieve and allow them the space to deal with the situation in their own way.

♦ Refrain from putting the father or mother down in front of the child. This is particularly important for childminders to remember. Never take sides. If you are speaking with the mother do not allow them to drag you into a negative discussion about their husband and vice versa.

There are always two sides to every story and it is not your place to be judgemental or apportion blame.

◆ Try to stick to usual routines as much as possible to avoid unnerving an already fragile child even more.

◆ Never ask questions of the child or use them as 'messengers'.

◆ With parental permission, notify the child's school in case of any possible distress suffered whilst they are at school so that teachers are aware of the situation.

After parents have separated or divorced there will be a period of grieving for all involved. This period of change involves rebuilding lives and moving ahead. It is an important time in which self esteem and confidence may well need to be repaired and parents may need your reassurance. There are no set rules on how things should develop and you may need to act as a 'go between' for a while in order to establish new routines. If you are asked to help with visits between ex-partners do so sensitively and with the child's best interests at heart.

OTHER KINDS OF SEPARATION

Although the word 'separation' automatically conjures up the idea of one parent leaving the other as in the case of a relationship break up, this is not always the case. Children may be separated from one or both of their parents for other reasons which can be equally as traumatic for them if not dealt with sensitively. Separation may result from:

◆ a lengthy stay in hospital either by the child or by one of the parents.

◆ one or both of the parents working away or perhaps being stationed abroad in the army. Sometimes children are sent to boarding school in these circumstances and may be separated from their parents during school term time;

◆ a parent may be in prison.

Children will cope with these types of situations differently and much again depends on their age and understanding of the situation, and whether they have been prepared for the separation. Ideally, the adults around them will have made plans whilst the separation is taking place. The adults may also be suffering from stress and anxiety, particularly in the case of a loved one being in hospital with a serious illness; and this can have a knock-on effect if not dealt with appropriately. Children who are separated from their parents or main carers will be affected by:

◆ their age and level of understanding;
◆ whether the separation was sudden or planned;
◆ the length of the separation;
◆ any previous history of separation in the child's life;
◆ their gender (studies have shown that boys are more distressed than girls by separation).

If at all possible, discuss separations with children, particularly planned separations, so that they are aware of what is happening and how long the situation is likely to go on for. Talk to them positively and allow them to keep in touch whenever possible by telephone, letter or, in the case of hospital stays, regular visits.

RE-MARRIAGE

So, the child has survived the separation and divorce of his or her parents and settled back into a happy routine, seeing both parents on a regular basis. How then, would you expect the child to react when one or both parents find new partners and plan to re-marry?

Although the exact number of people forming step-families is unknown, it is likely to be in the hundreds of thousands and research studies tell us that, after divorce, 50% of men will have remarried within two years and, after five years, 50% of women will have also remarried.

It is likely that the single most overwhelming feeling a child will experience in this type of situation is the uncertainty of his or her own position within the new family structure. When the parents separated but remained single it would probably have been easy for them to demonstrate the strength of their love and commitment to their child. However, as soon as another person comes onto the scene the child may see them as a potential threat intent on breaking up their happy routine. If recent years have been full of pain and insecurity before the parents divorced, it will take time for all involved to recover, and once a child has recovered from the past and moved on they may be very reluctant to allow someone else to come along and upset things for fear of repeating the pattern. It would be easy to assume that when a parent finds a new partner everything will be fine and the child and new partner will forge a special relationship. There are times when this is the case. However there are also many cases when things are not so easy. For example:

♦ The child may feel strong resentment towards their parent's new partner.

♦ The child's other parent may feel resentment towards the ex-partner and thrust their opinions onto the child; this may well be the case if the marriage break down was due solely to one parent's indiscretion.

♦ The parent's new partner may find it difficult to take on the care of someone else's child as they are unsure of their authority over another person's child.

♦ The parent's new partner may wish to adopt the role of the absent parent against the child's wishes; try to take mum/dad's place.

♦ There may be other children involved. A parent's new partner bringing step-children into the equation can have a devastating affect on a child.

BEREAVEMENT

Young children have a limited understanding of bereavement and may believe the situation to be short term. The words 'gone forever' are hard for most of us to comprehend so to expect a young child to accept them may be asking too much. The child may grieve for a long time and, when you begin to think they have finally accepted the situation, they may revert back and start to ask for the deceased person again. The death of a parent or close member of the family can have a devastating affect on a child and the situation needs to be handled with patience and sensitivity. Encourage the child to talk about the deceased person but do not force them to open up about their feelings until they are ready to do so. Answer their questions as openly and honestly as you can taking into account their age and level of understanding.

THE BIRTH OF A NEW BABY

Accepting the birth of a new baby can be very difficult for some children. Feelings of jealousy and insecurity may well surface. Single children who have not had to share their parents may experience feelings of rejection and become unsure of their parents' love for them. It can be particularly hard if the mother has a difficult birth and needs to stay in hospital or requires time to recuperate. An exhausted mother with a demanding baby may unintentionally appear to neglect the older child whilst she concentrates on her newborn.

Around 50–80% of new mothers suffer from the 'baby blues' when they understandably feel tired, stressed, anxious and weepy. This usually lasts for a few days after the birth and needs no special treatment. However, between 10–15% of women may suffer worse depression which can last weeks or even months after the birth of their baby. In these cases it is vital that they receive the support they need and, if you sense that a parent of one of the children you are caring for is going through this kind of experience, try to offer them as much time, support and reassurance as necessary and encourage them to seek medical advice.

It is vital that parents make time to be with their older offspring however tired or overwhelmed they may be feeling after the birth of a new baby. Encouraging older children to help with the care of the newborn will help them to accept the baby more quickly and give them a feeling of self-worth and helpfulness. Even young children can be included in the bathing and changing of a new baby, and by including your older children in these simple tasks you will help them to feel important and needed.

MOVING HOUSE

Moving house may not seem a very important or particularly eventful time in a child's life, however you should never underestimate the importance of familiar surroundings to a child. The security of a loving home is vital to a child's well being. Moving house is a stressful time for the adults in the family and this alone can bring anxiety to a child. If moving house does not involve moving a long distance then the disruption should be minimal as the child will not be too far from family, friends and familiar surroundings. However if the move means a change of school and leaving friends and family behind, it can have a devastating affect on a child. Some children may even liken the move to that of bereavement and may feel they will never see their friends again. Long-distance house moves must be dealt with sensitively. Try to explain things to the child and allow them as much time as possible to come to terms with the situation. If possible, make regular visits to their old friends particularly in the first few months when they may be finding it difficult to forge new friendships.

STARTING SCHOOL

Another important factor which may influence a child's behaviour is starting school. Some children absolutely adore school; from the very first moment they hang their coat up and walk into the classroom they are settled and at ease. Others may take weeks or even months before they are truly happy and settled. Every child is unique and how long it takes for them to settle into their school environment will be different.

Neither of my own two children enjoyed playgroup. Nursery was only slightly better, and when they first began at primary school, if I didn't leave them holding a teacher's hand, they would end up following me all the way back home! However, I must stress that their inability to settle into school quickly has by no means hindered their education and both are now happy, confident and bright young men! The stress I suffered when they started school was, I don't mind admitting, immense. Although I knew they were in safe hands and would come to no harm, my heart was often in my mouth as I left them with tears streaming down their faces in the capable hands of the teacher.

School is a big change for children who have been used to spending their early years at home with mum or dad. Admittedly in today's society, where a large number of parents return to work shortly after giving birth, the separation on a daily level starts when the child is still a baby and therefore both the parent and child have already become used to spending time away from one another before the time to begin school approaches. However, a child who has never been away from their parents until starting school or one who has spent limited time in day care may feel a huge wrench when they begin in full-time education.

You can help to ease children into school life slowly by visiting the school with them regularly in the months prior to them beginning. If you already take and collect older children they will be visiting with you anyway and you can use this time to explain where the various classrooms are and introduce them to some of the teachers so that they won't be quite so intimidated when the time comes for their own big day. Enlist the help of the older children you care for and ask them to look out for the new child who is starting. Encourage them to play together in the first few days whilst they are finding their feet and forging friendships of their own.

UNEMPLOYMENT

Unemployment can have a big impact on the way a child behaves. They may feel resentment if their parents are unemployed and money is tight. They may well see what their friends have to play with, see how they are dressed and listen to their tales of holidays and parties, and this can all make a child feel inadequate if their own parents are not in a position to provide them with the same. Being affluent, however, is not a measure of how loved and cherished a child is and parents who are unemployed and who may be struggling to bring their child up on limited money will still love their child very much. Love is not measured by material objects but children, unfortunately, may not see things this way and they may resort to thieving, bullying and lying in order to try to gain the possessions of their friends.

RACE, CULTURE AND RELIGION

It is important to remember that the way children behave in one culture may be completely unacceptable in other cultures. Every race, culture and religion has its own unique features that influence people. Behaviour is not the only issue which may be affected by cultural traditions and heritage, and we must think carefully about how our own views and values are affected.

Diversity is all about differences and we need to accept and embrace the fact that we are all different physically, socially, culturally, emotionally and sexually. Diversity stands for variety and we should all try to be tolerant of and respect and value the differences in today's society.

Although we are all different we all have the right to:

◆ equal respect;
◆ equal opportunity;
◆ equal justice.

CHILD ABUSE

It is important to understand that child abuse does not discriminate and it can happen in any family regardless of the family structure or parenting style. You must never assume that child abuse only happens to children in poor families or in single-parent families. It is just as likely to occur in respectable, affluent families and can result in severe psychological damage to a child which can affect them for the rest of their lives. Although it does not follow that abused children will automatically grow up to be abusers themselves, it is common for adults who have suffered abuse as children to find it difficult to form lasting relationships and they may even have problems when it comes to being parents to their own children.

There are four main types of abuse:

♦ neglect;
♦ physical abuse;
♦ sexual abuse;
♦ emotional abuse.

In most cases children who are abused suffer at the hands of someone they know and trust rather than a stranger. A child who is being abused may show both physical and behavioural signs. Identifying abuse in children is often very difficult as the child may become withdrawn and refuse to talk about their experiences. Sometimes the child may even lie in order to protect their abuser through misguided loyalty, particularly if the person who is abusing them is a respected member of their family or a close friend.

CONCLUDING POINTS

In addition to all these factors which can affect the way a child behaves we should also look carefully at our own opinions, views and expectations. You will undoubtedly have your own views on what is and is not an acceptable way for children to behave and these may well differ from the views of your friends, colleagues and the parents of the children you care for. What you yourself may be very tolerant of could prove totally unacceptable in someone else's family set-up and it is important, when caring for other people's children, that you accept the differences in the way people bring up their children.

The laws of this country set out what is acceptable to society in general and it is important that we teach children to grow up with the understanding that rules are there for the benefit of everyone and, whether we like it or not, we must abide by these rules to ensure that everyone has the right to a happy, safe existence.

Sometimes we may mistake aspects of a child's behaviour for naughtiness when, in fact they are just normal traits associated with the child's age. For example it is not 'naughty' for a young child to soil or wet themselves. A child's control over his or her bladder and bowel movements varies immensely from child to child, but it is fair to say that a child under the age of 18 months will have limited control over their muscles and will invariably experience 'accidents' from time to time. This is not being naughty. Likewise a child who cries, shows feelings of resentment or jealousy or who may accidentally inflict pain through curiosity, such as pulling hair, may be simply showing normal behaviour for their age.

5

Unwanted Behaviour

WHAT TRIGGERS UNACCEPTABLE BEHAVIOUR?

Sometimes children's behaviour falls short of our expectations. There are many reasons why this may happen. Below is a list of the most common, everyday causes of unwanted behaviour. By analysing and eliminating as many of the potential causes of unwanted behaviour as possible, we should be able to reduce the number of incidents when a child behaves inappropriately and deal with them more effectively when they do.

The child may feel:

◆ tired;
◆ hungry;
◆ bored;
◆ unwell;
◆ frightened;
◆ anxious;
◆ frustrated;
◆ restricted.

They may be:

◆ testing the limits or pushing boundaries to see how far adults and other children can be pushed;
◆ unaware of any potential dangers;
◆ exploring their environment;
◆ copying what they think others are doing;
◆ attention seeking;

- unable to control their emotions and feelings;
- feeling left out or treated unfairly;
- unsettled or confused.

Children may also show signs of unacceptable behaviour when they:

- do not understand what is expected of them;
- have a particular learning difficulty, allergy, etc;
- do not have clear, consistent boundaries to follow.

Although there may seem to be a lot of causes for unwanted behaviour and you may feel overwhelmed at the thought of having to deal with all these scenarios, it is worth bearing in mind that the majority of these causes can be eliminated with careful planning.

Tiredness and hunger

Let us look again at the eight causes in the first list. Tiredness and hunger can be dealt with relatively easily by allowing the child to sleep and offering food. Avoid allowing children to get to a point where lack of sleep and food is causing behavioural problems. Stick to planned routines for meals and naps.

Boredom

Boredom is often a trigger for unwanted behaviour and this can be avoided by providing the child with adequate toys and activities to stimulate them. Remember that a child does not always need expensive toys and games; *you* are the best toy a child can have. Make time for the children and have fun with them! Encourage them to use their imagination, involve them in activities suitable for their age and stage of development, and most importantly take into account their personal preferences. Remember, setting a task or activity which is too complex for the child's age is just as bad as not setting a task at all. The child will quickly lose interest in an activity that is too difficult for them to complete. Have realistic expectations of what the child can achieve and set your activities around their individual ability.

Include children in your own everyday tasks such as sorting the washing, setting the table, preparing simple meals and washing-up. Children love to be involved in 'adult' tasks and will enjoy helping you.

Illness

Illness can be another trigger for unacceptable behaviour and this is something you have little control over. A child who is feeling unwell may be irritable and unable to concentrate. You should make them as comfortable as possible, give them lots of love and affection and seek medical advice if necessary. A child who is unwell and unable to take part in activities or conduct themselves appropriately should not be in an early years setting. Contact parents if necessary and arrange for them to collect their child as soon as possible if you feel that they are not well enough to be in the setting.

Fear and anxiety

Feelings of fear and anxiety are often apparent in young children and can be caused by very simple things like a change in routine. Children need the security of a routine and sometimes even small changes can upset them. Whilst some children cope admirably with big changes such as starting playgroup or nursery, others take a while to settle in. You need to make sure that the child's confidence is boosted and give lots of praise and encouragement. Occasionally, even with careful planning, you cannot prevent a child from feeling scared or anxious. Events which are planned such as starting nursery or school should be talked about well in advance. Talk positively about the teachers, classroom, etc. and, if possible, arrange visits to the school prior to the child's first day so that they can be eased into the situation slowly and become familiar with their surroundings. Books can be very good for helping children become accustomed to the changes ahead.

Other factors which may cause fear or anxiety are not always so easy to prepare for. Thunderstorms, for example, are spontaneous and can occur without warning. Many young children are afraid of the loud noises of the thunder and they may become frightened and anxious.

Reassurance is needed when a child has these kinds of feelings and they should never be ridiculed because of their fears.

Frustration

Frustration can occur in anyone, at any age. As adults we try to control our frustration when we are confronted with bad service, poor driving, terrible weather, traffic jams, etc. However children are less able to show reason and when frustrated they tend to lose their temper and lash out. Frustration can be caused by a lack of ability to communicate. Children know what they want long before they are able to tell us and, if we fail to understand what they are trying to say to us, they can often become frustrated. Frustration often leads to tantrums. Taking the time to listen to the child and respond to their needs will help to eliminate these feelings.

Restriction

A child who is restricted may behave inappropriately. Children need space and freedom to run about and express themselves. A child who has been cooped up indoors all day, for example, may be full of pent-up energy bursting for release. Allow the child to play outside whenever possible. Children can play outside even in the winter months and, on particularly wet days, why not dress appropriately in waterproofs and Wellingtons and run through the puddles? The children will love it and there is no rule that says outdoor play is only for when the sun is shining!

Using common sense and looking at the needs and requirements of the child will enable you to successfully manage their behaviour. Planning ahead and anticipating their needs may eliminate the problems all together.

Now let us look at the second list. The eight triggers for unacceptable behaviour in this list are a little more complex and will require more management. The main reasons children resort to unwanted behaviour through one of these causes is down to their age and lack of understanding. There is little you can do about a child's age and level of understanding except to take solace in the fact that they will get older and grasp things better in time!

Testing the limits

Testing the limits and pushing boundaries is something that all children will do at some time. Making sure that children are aware of the rules will help to eliminate this problem. The 'grey' areas when parents collect their children from early years settings are often the times when children play up. They are unsure of who is in control at this point: their parent, childminder or nursery nurse, etc. The rules they have adhered to all day go out of the window and they begin to think they can do as they please. The child is effectively challenging their carer to comment on the behaviour they are showing whilst their parent is present. Ideally in this situation the parent will reprimand their own child, however there may be occasions when a child is doing something that *they* know is unacceptable but that the parent is not aware of. For example, if you do not allow children to climb on the furniture when a parent is not present do not let them do this the minute their parent walks through the door. They may be allowed to do many things at home which you will not allow in your own setting and children must learn the difference. *Never* ignore unacceptable behaviour just because a child's parent is present. This sends out the wrong message not just to the child who is misbehaving but to every other child present.

Unaware of danger

There may be occasions when a child behaves in a way that doesn't meet with the adults' expectations because they are unaware or do not realise the danger of the situation. For example a child who runs into the road does not do so because they are trying to get themselves knocked down by a car. They are doing so to attract adult attention and do not fully understand the danger of their actions. Making sure that a child is never in a dangerous situation is the way to avoid this cause of inappropriate behaviour. If a child insists on running into the road after the dangers have been explained then using a restraint such as reins or a wrist strap will prevent this behaviour from happening again until the child is able to accept the situation.

Exploring their environment

Children may also exhibit unacceptable behaviour when exploring their surroundings. Children are, by nature, inquisitive and they like to explore their environment. They should be allowed to explore whenever possible, however it is your duty to ensure that the environment around them is safe and suitable for such exploration. Remove any potential hazards such as ornaments and vases on low tables and ensure they can not push things into power sockets, video recorders, etc.

Watching and copying

Children learn through watching and copying. Is a child really being naughty when he pulls up tulips after watching you weed the garden? Can we really expect a three year-old to know the difference between a weed and a plant? In such cases children should be allowed to explore the garden, help you to plant seeds and flowers, pull up weeds, etc. but they should do so under supervision. Explain to them what you are doing and why and show them which plants to care for and which to dispose of.

Remember that whilst children will imitate our good behaviour and traits they will also copy our bad behaviour, and it is up to us to provide them with a positive role model at all times.

Attention seeking

Attention seeking behaviour can often be a way for children to get noticed. A child who is playing well and appears engrossed in an activity can all too often be overlooked. If a child is exhibiting attention seeking behaviour is this because 'bad' behaviour is the only way he or she gets any attention? If so then you must look carefully at how you treat the children. Praise and reward the children who are showing pleasing behaviour and lavish attention on *them* rather than on the child who is behaving inappropriately.

Unable to control emotions

Young children are often unable to control their emotions and feelings. They may become angry and lash out or cry for seemingly trivial reasons. Children need to be encouraged to explore their feelings and emotions and talk about the way they are feeling. Always ensure that the child knows they can talk to you but never pressurise them into opening up if they do not want to. Do not laugh at or ridicule a child who gets upset or angry but offer reassurance.

Feeling left out or treated unfairly

Sometimes children can get angry and frustrated if they are feeling left out or consider that they are being unfairly treated. Patience is not something that most children are good at showing and they often find it hard to wait their turn or to share. Explain to the child that they are not being left out but, like everyone else, they need to wait their turn. Keep an eye on group activities which do not include an adult and make sure that no-one is being overlooked. Groups of three can often cause problems as one person inevitably feels left out. Encourage activities which include everyone and show children how to share and take turns.

Unsettled or confused

A child who is experiencing lots of change in their family circumstances or is new to the setting may be feeling unsettled and confused. These feelings, like most emotions, can be very powerful and may even frighten a child who is experiencing them. Reassure the child as much as possible and make them feel welcome and valued. Give the child as much one to one attention as possible and encourage them to take part in simple activities. Take your cue from the child and never force them to take part in anything they are not happy doing. Children will often sit and watch others for some time before finding the confidence to join in.

The final three causes which may result in unwanted behaviour are a little more difficult to deal with and may take some time to implement. This is because the issues may be due to the age and understanding of the child or they may be out of your control.

Not understanding expectations

If a child does not understand what is expected of them this may be for several reasons:

1. They lack communication skills.
2. The adults around them may be using language which is too complex for their stage of development or is not clear enough.
3. They have not been told what is expected.

In these cases it is important for the adults to explain in simple terms, appropriate to the child's age and level of understanding, what is acceptable and what is not. Positive childcare is all about bringing out the best in the child. It is important that the adults around then listen, understand, praise and encourage them. Try to refrain from pointing out where a child is going wrong and instead concentrate on rewarding and praising the things they get right.

Children with particular learning difficulties will have little or no control over their behaviour and the way they respond to some things. Depending on the nature of the problem you may need to seek additional help from professionals. Children may be suffering from:

1. speech or language problems;
2. sensitivity to food additives which result in irritability, aggression and being unable to concentrate;
3. Attention Deficit with Hyperactivity Disorder (ADHD);
4. Attention Deficit Disorder (ADD).

SETTING BOUNDARIES

All children need boundaries. Boundaries put a limit on behaviour and enable a child to understand what is acceptable and what is not. Boundaries help a child to feel safe and secure. It is, however, not enough to simply set boundaries; it is essential that *everyone* is aware of and understands them. It is important to be realistic when setting boundaries and you must take into account the child's age and level of understanding. There is little point in having a rule which states that all children must ask before going to the toilet if the children in your particular setting are in nappies. Avoid complicated rules and making a fuss over trivial things.

Most children and adults will accept the need for boundaries and in order to make them effective we need to consider the following factors:

◆ Are the boundaries realistic?
◆ Are the boundaries fair?
◆ How are the children made aware of the boundaries?
◆ How are the adults made aware of the boundaries?
◆ Do the adults agree with the boundaries?

Children who do not have clear, consistent boundaries will inevitably display unwanted behaviour mainly due to the fact that they are unsure of what is expected of them. It can be very confusing for a child if they think that what may be acceptable one day could well be unacceptable the next.

TIP

All children need boundaries. Exactly what limits you choose for your own setting will depend largely on the age and level of understanding of the children you care for, but it may be worth bearing the following in mind:

◆ Try not to give in to children in the long-term in search of short-term peace and quiet. This very rarely pays off.
◆ Remember that you are stronger than the child. Learn to cope with their behaviour and ride it out.
◆ Children need the adults in their lives to take charge, even if they do not know it themselves. They need to learn and try out new experiences from a safe place and within safe boundaries.
◆ Bear in mind that children will test your patience and try to push limits in order to find out how far you are willing to go.

POLICIES

Most early years settings have a policy with regard to behaviour. Childminders are no exception to this rule and are advised to have a policy stating exactly what is and is not acceptable in the setting. A policy should be written clearly and the contents shared with the children and their parents. A copy of the policy should be given to each parent and also displayed on the walls of the setting.

Behaviour policies are usually based on simple 'house rules' which are put in place to protect everyone in the setting. Remember to be realistic and avoid setting very high expectations that most children will struggle to reach.

Establishing a successful framework for behaviour will depend on:

◆ Your ability to encourage the children to learn your rules by reminding them frequently.

◆ Your ability to use clear, precise language and give simple instructions.

◆ Your ability to explain to the children why you have rules and what will happen if they are not met.

Your own behaviour policy will depend on what you view as unacceptable behaviour. For example, some people may not mind if children roam around their house wearing their outdoor shoes while others may insist that they are taken off at the door. Figures 2 and 3 show examples of what behaviour policies in a childminding setting may look like.

BEHAVIOUR POLICY

Kindness costs nothing
Include others in your games
Never do to others what you wouldn't like done to you
Don't tell tales
Never tell lies
Expect consequences if rules are broken
Smacking others will not be tolerated
Swearing and bad manners are not permitted

Fig. 2. Example behaviour policy for older children.

Biting and kicking is not nice
Expect to be punished when you misbehave
Good behaviour will be rewarded
Outdoor shoes must be removed
Outside is for running – not indoors
Don't tell lies

Fig. 3. Example behaviour policy for younger children.

Obviously the policy in Figure 2 was written with older children in mind as the wording would be too complex for young children. The policy has been written to look attractive and encourage people to read it and take notice. A policy written for younger children may read something like Figure 3. Use words like 'please' and 'thank you' rather than more complex words like 'manners' which most young children will not understand.

STICKING TO THE RULES

There is absolutely no point whatsoever in creating a framework for behaviour and writing a behaviour policy if you do not stick to the rules you have set out. What is the point of writing a policy which clearly states 'remove outdoor shoes before entering' if you allow children to run through your house with their Wellingtons on? A policy is not simply a way of decorating the walls. It should provide useful information that *everyone* understands and abides by.

TIP

Remember that rules need to be:

◆ simple but fair;
◆ kept to a minimum;
◆ of a nature that young children can understand;
◆ consistent;
◆ changed to take into account a child's changing age and development.

When we say 'no' to a child it is important that we mean 'no'. Most children will respond to this expression provided it is used *sparingly*. If you constantly tell a child they cannot do something when in fact there is no real reason for you to say 'no', then it will have little impact on them. Set your rules and stick to them. If a child thinks that they can bend the rules by being uncooperative or by wearing you down with tantrums and whinging then, rest assured, this is the behaviour they will resort to. For a behaviour framework to work you must be fair but firm.

The following suggestions may be useful for dealing with children's unwanted behaviour.

♦ **Be optimistic**. Persevere and adopt a sense of humour.

♦ **Be clear**. Decide what you want the children to do and explain your expectations to them clearly with language they can relate to.

♦ **Be firm**. If a child fails to abide by your rules do not give up. Insist on the type of behaviour you expect and show appreciation when the child has achieved it. Withhold your praise by walking away or ignoring the behaviour if the child behaves badly.

♦ **Be consistent**. To carry any kind of authority in a childcare setting you need to be determined. If a child thinks they can wear you down they will! Always be prepared to follow through with your sanctions and then everyone will know that you mean what you say. Consistent boundaries have the added bonus of adding to a child's sense of security.

♦ **Be prepared**. Try to work out a suitable strategy for dealing with ongoing problems. Never wait until the problem has got out of hand before doing something about it.

♦ **Be available**. Show the children that you are interested in them and that you value their views and opinions. Adults are very important to children and it is important for both children and childminders to form close relationships and to spend quality time doing activities together.

◆ **Be human**. Try not to set your expectations of children so high that they have difficulty achieving them. Admit when you are wrong and give rewards and punishments that are appropriate but not excessive.

Although it is important to establish boundaries and to make sure that children are aware of what you will and will not accept it is equally important that you ensure that when a child behaves unacceptably it is *the behaviour you do not like, not the child.*

Some procedures are completely unacceptable when managing children's behaviour and should never be used. Unacceptable procedures for behaviour management include:

1. using any form of physical punishment including smacking, pinching, shaking, prodding or rough handling;
2. shouting;
3. criticism or comparison;
4. name calling;
5. humiliation;
6. isolation.

TIP

When dealing with unwanted behaviour always:

◆ Stay calm.
◆ Speak clearly and firmly without shouting.
◆ Think carefully before you speak.
◆ Use the simplest and least restrictive approach.

TANTRUMS

Many young children resort to tantrums as a means of trying to win over a situation to get their own way. They wrongly believe that by throwing themselves on the floor, lashing out, screaming and shouting they will get what they want. Tantrums are often embarrassing for adults and it is because of their embarrassment that they give in and succumb to the child's demands. This is the worst thing an adult can do. Agreeing to the child's demands may well put a stop to the tantrum at that time, but it effectively tells the child that if they create a scene they will get their own way. Tantrums will become common practice for children if they think they will win! The best way of dealing with a tantrum is to ignore it. Stick to your rules despite the child's behaviour and *never* be tempted to give in just to avoid a tantrum.

Around 50% of all two year-olds have tantrums on a regular basis – hence the term the 'terrible twos'. Tantrums usually occur in the presence of a parent or carer such as a childminder or relative. Children rarely resort to tantrums in a playgroup, nursery or school environment.

The main cause for tantrums is frustration:

◆ They can't have or do what they want.
◆ They are being criticised.
◆ They feel they are being treated unfairly.

The main need for tantrums is to seek attention and to vent anger.

It sometimes seems as if a child has 'blown up' for no reason at all because the behaviour immediately prior to the tantrum appears to be trivial. Often though, it is this last 'trivial' occurrence which is all that is needed to set off a tantrum that the child has in fact been building up to. Tantrums may vary in severity but there is no mistaking the fact that the underlying feeling being expressed is 'anger'!

There appears to be three important points which you should remember in order to avoid temper tantrums:

◆ Be clear about your rules and never leave an opportunity open for misinterpretation. Tell the child exactly what they can and cannot do.

◆ Listen to what the child is telling you and act upon this whenever possible. If there is no alternative, for example if you are waiting at a bus stop for the bus to arrive and the child is getting impatient, then explain to them that they have no alternative. Try to make the wait less boring by playing a game, for example.

◆ Avoid trying to 'control' the child. Instead try to help them feel as though they are in control by allowing as much freedom of choice as possible.

The best methods for dealing with tantrums are:

◆ Distract or divert the child.
◆ Ignore the behaviour.
◆ Walk away from the child.

Of course these methods are not always possible, for example if you are in a public place it may not be an option to walk away from the child. At times like this you should:

◆ Hold the child.
◆ Reassure the child.
◆ Offer hugs and cuddles.

Remember that tantrums can be a frightening experience for a child. When a child is experiencing a tantrum you should never:

◆ Smack them.
◆ Shake them.
◆ Handle them roughly.

These responses can be harmful. When the tantrum is over it is important to talk to the child. Encourage them to talk about their feelings and offer reassurance in order to discourage a repeat of the behaviour. If you are caring for someone else's child you should inform them if the tantrum is particularly severe. Remember, NEVER allow a child to manipulate you through tantrums. It may alleviate the problem initially but, rest assured, by giving in to the child to curb one tantrum you will increase the frequency of further tantrums.

TIP

The following is a checkpoint for coping with tantrums:

- Stay calm yourself no matter how angry or embarrassed the child makes you feel. Losing your own temper will just fuel the child's tantrum and add to the problem.
- Let the child know that you are not pleased by telling them what aspect of their behaviour is unacceptable.
- Remove the child from the situation.
- Explain to the child that they can return to what they were doing previously but only when they have calmed down and begun to behave sensibly again.
- Restrain children when necessary in order to prevent them from hurting themselves or others.

Remember, temper tantrums are normal and do not usually lead to serious problems. As the child gets older they will learn to deal more effectively with the stresses of everyday life and become much calmer.

BRIBERY

Bribery is often mistaken for reward. Giving a child a reward for good behaviour is *not* the same as bribing the child to behave well. Bribery should not be used in order to get a child to behave. I am sure that most parents have, at some point, fallen into the trap of saying to their child, 'If you are good whilst we are shopping today I will buy you some sweets/a book/a toy' or whatever. In essence this is not a problem; however problems will arise when a child will only behave *if* they are promised a bribe. Never allow a child to use bribery on you. For example do not allow them to tell you they will behave only if you buy them a toy/sweets, etc. Children should be encouraged to behave well because they want to, not because of the reward they may receive.

TIP

Much as it is always nicer for a child if they are allowed choices, there will be times when you are not in a position to offer a choice and you will need to give a command. When giving commands always:

◆ Give one command at a time – do not inundate children with lots of orders as this will confuse and overwhelm them.

◆ Be realistic – always make sure that the child is capable of doing what you ask of them; take into account their age and ability.

◆ Avoid threatening children and try to use *positive* rather than *negative* language.

◆ Repeat the command to reiterate what you expect from the child.

◆ Explain clearly and precisely what you expect from the child.

◆ Allow the child sufficient time to complete the command.

BULLYING

What is a bully? The definition of a bully is an adult or child who deliberately intimidates of persecutes someone with the intention of causing them distress.

Bullying can be either physical, social, psychological or verbal and take the form of:

◆ punching;
◆ hitting;
◆ kicking;
◆ teasing;
◆ name calling;
◆ sarcasm;
◆ hair pulling;
◆ racial remarks;
◆ damaging of property;
◆ intimidation;
◆ theft of possessions;
◆ threatening behaviour;
◆ exclusion – refusal to allow others to participate in activities.

You may be in the unfortunate position of caring for a child who is being bullied or who is in fact doing the bullying themselves. Both the victim and the bully need support. Although bullying is rare among children under the age of five years, once a child starts school they may become the victim of name calling and fighting.

Bullying – the facts
- Bullying is a shameful part of our culture.
- Bullying can happen anywhere: at home, school or work.
- Bullying is not always physical and violent, it can also be emotional and subtle.
- Bullying is a secret problem and victims often try to hide their suffering.
- Bullying can have long lasting effects on the lives of the victims and they may carry the scars with them throughout their adult lives.
- Bullying can lead to suicide.

The bully
A bully is often hostile and aggressive with issues of their own. They may feel inadequate and unable to cope with their own problems, resulting in them causing distress to others. Bullies nearly always pick victims which are weaker and less powerful than themselves. Bullies may work alone, in pairs or in a group, and are intent on causing pain and distress to their victims.

Victims are not always children. The elderly, infirm and less able members of our society are also vulnerable to bullying. As responsible adults we have a duty to tackle bullying and as childcare practitioners we have a responsibility towards children, alongside parents and schools, to protect them from this kind of behaviour.

Many factors can cause a child to become a bully and their behaviour usually arises because they have suffered a set back or specific problem in their own lives. Bullying can arise from boredom, insecurity, frustration or a lack of or inability to make friends. It is easy to fall into the trap of believing that children who bully come from disadvantaged backgrounds with little or no parental input or support;

however this is not always true. Sometimes children from very affluent, loving families who have been lavished with attention may become accustomed to having everything their own way and relish the feeling of power that bullying gives them.

Whatever the reason for a child to resort to bullying, there is usually an underlying reason for their behaviour and, whilst we cannot condone their actions, it is important that we take the time to try to understand why they are behaving in this way and to offer them help and support. It has been suggested that a child who bullies is more likely to grow up aggressive, to forge poor relationships and possibly even become an abuser. It is for this reason, therefore, that the bully's behaviour must not be ignored.

Children who resort to bullying may:

♦ have very low self-esteem;
♦ not believe in their own self-worth;
♦ not be encouraged to show their feelings;
♦ be afraid of failure;
♦ have experienced some form of bullying or abuse themselves.

As a childcare practitioner you need to:

♦ Stay calm.
♦ Help the child to build their self-esteem.
♦ Value the child and their achievements.
♦ Talk to the child (with parental permission) to discuss their actions, and try to establish whether they themselves are experiencing problems which results in them bullying.
♦ Be there for the child if they want to talk.
♦ Agree with the child's parents and school on a strategy to deal with the behaviour.

Bullying can take many forms and it can be very upsetting and stressful for the person being bullied. Whilst bullying itself is a form of unacceptable behaviour, problems can increase when the child who is being bullied also resorts to unacceptable behaviour as a way of coping with the problems they are facing.

The victim

It can sometimes be very difficult to recognise when a child is being bullied. Whilst some children can cope well in the face of adversity and may shrug off name calling and hair pulling, others may become extremely distressed. Very often the stress felt by a child who is being bullied manifests itself in changes in the way they normally behave, and it is these changes which must be recognised and acted upon to prevent serious repercussions. Tragically, some children who are experiencing bullying feel there is no one to talk to and nowhere to turn and these victims become so desperate that they end up taking their own lives. We need to prevent this from happening by recognising and dealing with the bully and offering the victim support and understanding.

Firstly, we need to be aware of changes in a child's behaviour which may be the result of possible bullying:

- refusal to go to school/nursery;
- crying for no apparent reason;
- unexplained injuries;
- ripped clothing;
- complaints of illness such as tummy ache and head ache in the hope of avoiding going to school/nursery;
- being physically sick;
- often appearing hungry (this could be a sign of having had their lunch or lunch money taken from them by the bully);
- aggressive behaviour;
- disturbed sleep;
- regression – thumb sucking, comfort behaviour, etc.;
- bed wetting;
- suffering from nightmares;
- frequently 'losing' possessions;
- asking for or stealing money;
- becoming withdrawn;

- refusing to eat;
- attempting to harm themselves;
- deterioration in school work.

This list is extensive but is by no means exhaustive. Just as someone who resorts to bullying does so for a number of reasons, the results of a bully's actions are also many and varied.

If a child you are caring for is being bullied, or you suspect that they are being bullied, you must take action. *Never* ignore it or put it down to growing up – something to be endured which will fizzle out when the bully finds someone else to pick on. No one should have to suffer at the hands of a bully and the situation needs to be carefully monitored and rectified. If a child confides in you that they are being bullied do not tell them that you will keep it to yourself, which may well be a condition of their disclosure, as you will be unable to help them if you keep what they are telling you a secret. You can, however, make sure that you only talk to those who need to know such as the child's parents and teachers.

Always make sure you get the facts and try to check that the child is not unintentionally provoking the bullying through anti-social behaviour.

Whilst offering help and support to the victim of bullying it is also a good idea to encourage them to take positive steps towards preventing bullying. Sometimes a child can inadvertently give the impression that they are a victim, and we can encourage them to look at their own behaviour and help them to protect themselves and avoid becoming vulnerable to bullying. This may involve:

- helping to build self-esteem and self-worth;
- helping the child to build friendships;
- encouraging the child to talk about any problems they are facing;
- helping the child to understand that they are not to blame for the bully's behaviour.

Seeking help and support

One of the most important things for the victim of bullying to know is that they can turn to you for help and support. Bottling up their feelings and not having anyone to turn to may make an already difficult situation intolerable. Children need to know that there is someone available that they can rely on, someone who will give impartial advice and who will know what to do when they are experiencing problems.

As a childcare practitioner you may have children confiding in you because they are unable or unwilling to talk to their parents. You must make it clear that if they won't tell their parents about the bullying they are experiencing then *you* will. It is important that the main carers in a child's life are aware of any issues their child has and that they work together to find a solution. You can provide the child and their parents with the help and support they need to see them through times of bullying by:

◆ having a good knowledge of child development and how this can be affected by bullying i.e. changes in behaviour etc.;

◆ encouraging trusting relationships between the child, their parents and yourself;

◆ showing empathy and understanding.

WHat childminders and parents can do in the event of bullying

◆ Initially talk to the child to ascertain whether or not your suspicions of bullying are well-founded.

◆ Take what the child tells you seriously and never tell them to 'toughen up' or ridicule their predicament.

◆ Tell the child that you love them and care about them and that you will do everything you can to sort things out. They need to know that you are on their side 100%.

- Reassure them that they are not to blame for the bullying they are experiencing.

- Explain that crying or responding to the bullies can actually encourage them. Bullies like to see how upset their victims are and it is this type of response that they are aiming for.

- Help the child to be prepared for the bully's taunts; with responses ready they may feel a little more in control.

- Work out, with the child, ways of minimising opportunities for the bullying to take place. For example, trying to avoid being alone – there is safety in numbers.

- Encourage the child to give the bully what they demand to avoid violence. Staying safe is more important than hanging onto money or possessions. Make sure the child knows that they must *tell* someone if they have been threatened and forced to hand over money or possessions.

- Make time to talk to the child and, more importantly, *listen* to them. They need to know you are there for them and they are not dealing with the situation on their own.

- Help the child to feel valued and important by giving them responsibilities whilst they are with you.

- Help the child to feel good about themselves. Bullying strips a child of their self-esteem and self-worth and they begin to feel useless and deserving of the misery they are feeling. Make the time to praise the child and tell them how much you care about them.

- Make diversions so that the child is not allowed to dwell on the problems and mope around. Encourage them to make new friends away from the area they are being bullied. Joining clubs are an excellent way of doing this.

WHAT SCHOOLS CAN DO IN THE EVENT OF BULLYING

Today it is compulsory for all schools to have an Anti-Bullying Policy. However it is important to remember that the school alone cannot be made responsible for sorting out the problem, and success can only be guaranteed if *everyone* works together. Schools must deal with any bullying incident in accordance with the procedures set out in their policy. Children, staff and parents should all be made aware of what will happen if bullying occurs. The school should be prepared to:

- Take the problem seriously.
- Carry out an investigation into the incident.
- Interview both the bully and the victim separately.
- Seek out and interview any witnesses.
- Decide on the most appropriate action. This will vary depending on the nature and level of severity of the bullying. It may mean:
  - obtaining an apology from the bully;
  - informing the bully's parents;
  - imposing sanctions on the bully;
  - seeking compensation for the victim from the bully;
  - providing information/lessons to the pupils in the school to make them aware of bullying and how they can help prevent it;
  - providing support within the school for the victim. This may consist of a teacher being assigned to the child for them to talk to if necessary.
- Provide follow up meetings with the victim's parents to report on the progress.
- Inform all members of staff about the bullying incidents and what action has been taken.
- Keep written records of the incident and the action taken.

Assertiveness

Both bullies and victims can learn a lot from trying out assertiveness techniques. Basic self-assertiveness training can help *everyone* feel better about themselves. It can teach you different ways of responding to awkward or upsetting situations.

There are three styles of response:

- passive;
- aggressive;
- assertive.

Passive

A person who is said to be passive allows other people to behave as if their needs and rights are more important than theirs. Passive people tend to consider themselves to be less important than others.

Aggressive

A person who is said to be aggressive behaves as though they are more important than others and that their rights matter more than those of others.

Assertive

A person who is said to be assertive respects themselves and others equally.

Broadly speaking, victims tend to be passive whilst bullies tend to be aggressive.

Self-assertiveness when making requests

- Decide what you want and be firm. 'I would like my books back.'
- Be short and precise when asking for something back.
- Plan ahead and be ready for situations before they arise.
- Practise what to say and do.

Self-assertiveness when dealing with insults and teasing

- Try responding with insults. Give the bully a taste of their own medicine.
- Try ignoring the insults and taunts – bullies are often looking for a response and when they don't get one they may get bored.

Dealing with anger

◆ Learn to recognise what makes you angry. Look for the signs of when you are going to 'explode' and be ready with a strategy to deal with these types of situations.

◆ Take deep breaths.

◆ Count to ten.

◆ Remove yourself from the situation or the person who is making you feel angry. Far from 'running away', this is the best strategy for avoiding conflict and arguments.

◆ Let off steam in other ways – exercise, kick a ball, etc.

◆ Relax – anger often stems from stress and anxiety. Learn to relax and control your temper.

Bullying policies

Bullying should never be ignored. It is a very serious issue which can vary considerably in severity and the response it provokes. Some schools and childcare settings have developed a separate policy relating specifically to bullying in addition to their behaviour policy. A policy on bullying may look like this:

BULLYING POLICY

In order for all children to feel valued in my setting and to enjoy their time here it is important that everyone understands my rules regarding bullying. I will NOT tolerate:

◆ Name calling and verbal abuse

◆ Fighting

◆ Physical attacks of any kind

◆ Threatening behaviour

◆ Racial or discriminatory remarks

◆ Exclusion of one child by another

Fig. 4. Example of a bullying policy.

6

Encouraging Positive Behaviour

It is all too easy, when we think about children's behaviour, to simply focus on the 'bad' behaviour – the unwanted behaviour that we are trying to discourage. Most children behave in a reasonable way a lot of the time but often this 'acceptable' behaviour is overlooked. It is therefore not surprising for children to misbehave at some time, especially if this kind of behaviour results in attention from an adult. 'Any attention is better than no attention at all' in a child's mind, and if by misbehaving a child gets noticed more than when they are behaving well then you are asking for trouble!

TIP

Remember – 'Behaviour noticed is behaviour repeated'. Rest assured that a child who receives lots of attention when they misbehave will continue to repeat their behaviour. Try ignoring unwanted behaviour and praising and rewarding children who are behaving well.

Encouraging children to behave and rewarding good behaviour is a better approach to managing a child's behaviour than having to administer punishments when they have misbehaved.

If we are really striving to find what is best for the child then we should be aiming to teach them skills for disciplining themselves. We should be encouraging them to compromise voluntarily rather than by force, and to achieve this we first need to set the child a good example.

We all need some form of self-discipline. As an adult we have learned what society demands and are aware of what is and is not socially acceptable. By having high standards ourselves and setting a good example at all times we can encourage children to follow suit.

All children strive to be accepted. They are searching for love, affection and approval from the adults in their lives and they must learn that they will not achieve this by being selfish, destructive or angry.

EMPOWERMENT

Getting a child to conform to what we require is often a battle of wills. The more we insist the child does something, the more they may dig their heels in and refuse. Children can be very stubborn and often a small disagreement can escalate into a crisis if the adult and child are at loggerheads. For example, young children rarely understand the concept of time and being late and in a rush is of little consequence to them. I have witnessed harassed parents and unhappy children at the school gates after a battle to get ready on time. The parent has to go to work, the children need to be at school and prior to that everyone needs to get washed, dressed and have breakfast. A child who refuses to co-operate in the morning rush can set the whole day up for disaster. Compromises need to be made by everyone. However, children do not want to be 'controlled'. Instead try offering choices and allow the child to make their own decisions rather than giving orders. Allow yourself plenty of time and, if necessary, get up 15–30 minutes earlier to ensure a relaxed, unrushed start to the day.

POSITIVE ROLE MODELS

Childminders, and indeed parents, should be aiming to send positive messages to children at all times. This is not always easy especially if a child is being particularly difficult. However you should think before you give a *request*, in order to avoid giving a *command*. You will find that a child responds much better to being asked politely to do something rather than being ordered, in very much the same way as an adult does. Rather than saying 'No' or 'Don't', try saying 'Why don't we...' or 'Let's do this...'. Explain the reasons behind your request. If you want the children to help you to tidy up, explain to them why. Try saying, 'Let's tidy up those toys together so that we don't fall over them', instead of saying 'Tidy those toys up'. Children will respond to this kind of request willingly in most cases, and you will achieve what you set out to without a battle.

Giving a child the opportunity to be in control of the situation, work things out and choose for themselves is called *empowerment*. In order for us to empower a child we must help them to develop confidence and positive self-esteem to enable them to manage their own behaviour. We need to listen to children carefully for this to be successful. We need to be aware of what they are saying verbally together with the information they give us through their actions, expressions and body language.

When encouraging empowerment it is important not to offer too many choices. Young children will be confused if you say, 'What would you like to play with?' This opens up a huge variety of activities which could make the child feel overwhelmed. Instead say something like, 'Would you like to play with the play dough or do you prefer to paint?' This narrows the choice down dramatically whilst still allowing the child freedom of choice. Older children can, of course, be offered a wider choice and should be allowed to make more complex decisions. Providing children with simple tasks, suitable to their age and level of understanding also helps a child to feel empowered.

It is vital that childminders understand that the most important people in a child's lives are their parents or carers. Children learn by watching and copying others, and it is with this in mind that we must always strive to offer them a positive role model at all times. A role model who is aggressive and abusive will not set a good example to a child and the chances are the child will copy this kind of behaviour. It is human nature for us all to get angry, upset, confused and annoyed at some point and no one is expecting you to be perfect all of the time. However, by thinking about our actions and controlling our feelings and temper whilst in the company of children we will be setting a good example. Show children how *you* cope in adverse situations and teach them how to control their anger and overcome their emotions.

Positive behaviour in children can be encouraged in several ways and Figure 5 shows some of the main methods.

Fig. 5. Encouraging positive behaviour in children.

Adults need to work at encouraging positive behaviour in children and there are several ways to achieve this.

Calm environment
A busy, hectic environment can be chaotic and result in stress for both children and adults. Adults under pressure can unintentionally pass their feelings onto children. A controlled, relaxed atmosphere will have benefits for everyone. Plan a workable routine and stick to it as far as possible. Incorporate quiet times for children to sit and read or talk about the day's events. Your days should not be one hectic mad rush but should include time for rest and reflection.

Empowerment
We have looked at empowering the child earlier in this chapter. Children should be allowed opportunities to enable them to be in control of situations. This is particularly useful for encouraging positive behaviour in older children.

Individual attention
Reward a child's good behaviour by telling them how pleased you are with them. A child who is given lots of adult attention will not need to resort to unwanted behaviour to be noticed.

REWARDS

It is important that we do not mistake giving rewards with bribery. It is possible to reinforce positive behaviour that we would like repeated with praise and rewards, and this method works well with most children. Think about your own behaviour. It can be particularly pleasing when someone congratulates you on a job well done and, whilst you may not actually receive a 'reward', the praise alone can be sufficient to boost your confidence and make you want to repeat the experience. Children should be treated in much the same way. Boosting their confidence with praise can be very effective. Praise should be used frequently when caring for young children although rewards can also be used when a child has behaved particularly well.

It is important to remember that whilst praise should be forthcoming whenever it is due, rewards should be kept to a minimum. If you start giving out rewards every time a child has said 'thank you', for example, they will come to expect it too often, under-valuing the reward itself. Rewards should be kept for special treats to acknowledge *exceptional* behaviour. Getting the balance right between praise and reward is not always easy, however you must make sure that rewards do not become so important to the child that praise alone is a disappointment.

Things to remember when using praise and rewards
- **Praise children frequently**. Showing children you are pleased with their behaviour will help to encourage positive behaviour.

- **Explain to children why they are being rewarded or praised**. It is of little help to a child who has shown particularly good behaviour to be given a reward at the end of the day whilst being told he has 'been a good boy today'. There will no doubt have been times when his behaviour has been less acceptable, and he may have forgotten that he waited patiently for his turn or helped to tidy the toys away without being prompted by the time the reward is given. Aim to praise a child and give any rewards at the *actual* time they are displaying positive behaviour to reiterate why they are being praised. For example, a child who has waited for his turn whilst playing a game might be praised by you saying, 'Good boy, Jacob, you can choose the story today for waiting patiently for your turn'. By praising the child and telling them what you are particularly pleased about you are helping *all* the children to understand what is expected of them.

♦ **Make sure that you choose your rewards carefully**. A full bag of sweets used as a reward for a child who has said 'please' or 'thank you' would be inappropriate, however one sweet or a sticker would work well.

Types of rewards

Although it is easy to praise a child when they are showing signs of appropriate behaviour, it is often more difficult to choose appropriate rewards. You must make sure that you do not over indulge children so that they simply act in a certain way just to gain a large reward. It is also important to avoid jealousy amongst other children who perhaps find it more difficult to earn rewards. Figure 6 shows examples of appropriate rewards.

Sweets

Rewards do not necessarily have to be sweets. In fact I would recommend that childminders seek the opinion and approval of the child's parent before giving sweets as a reward. Some parents do not like their children to have sweets and therefore by giving sweets as a reward for good behaviour you may unintentionally give the wrong message to the child. Being allowed something which is 'off limits' at home for being good elsewhere is not an effective way of promoting positive behaviour. Try substituting sweets for healthy food such as grapes, carrot sticks, celery, raisins, etc.

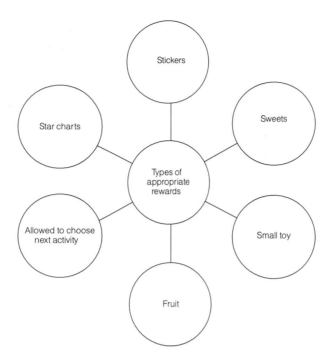

Fig. 6. Types of appropriate rewards.

Small toys

Rewarding a child with a small toy should not be a regular practice as, apart from the expense, the child may come to expect a gift every time they have behaved well. Children should be encouraged to behave well because they *want* to not simply because they are aiming for a present. Small toys could however be useful to reward a child's behaviour if they have behaved well during times of adversity or if their routine has been particularly disrupted, for example in the case of the birth of a new baby or when starting school. If you buy a gift for the child's new sibling it might be a good idea to buy a token gift for the big brother/sister to encourage them to welcome the baby and help to care for them. Young children can often feel pushed out when mum gives birth and, when lots of attention is heaped on the newborn, the older child can feel neglected.

Childminders may like to consider rewarding school-aged children with a token gift at the end of each term to show their appreciation for the good behaviour displayed. This ensures that the children need to show acceptable behaviour over a period of several weeks.

Allowed to choose the next activity

A child who has shown patience waiting their turn or has been particularly good at sharing may be rewarded by allowing them to choose the next activity or story, or allowing them an extra turn. Rewards like these make the child feel special and their behaviour valued. These types of rewards cost nothing and are easy to implement.

Stickers

Stickers are an excellent way of rewarding a child for specific behaviour and can easily take the place of sweets/fruit. Stickers can be awarded directly to the child for 'trying really hard at that task' or for 'painting a beautiful picture'. The child has received something they can show to their parents, as well as being praised for their work.

Star charts

Many people find that star or reward charts work particularly well for managing children's behaviour. These charts can be used both at home and at the childminder's house. Working in partnership with parents is vital when encouraging positive behaviour in children. A reward chart may look something Figure 7.

Stars can be added to the chart every time a child has shown positive behaviour. The stars can then be added up at the end of each week to calculate who has been awarded the most. The person with the most stars should be praised and may even be rewarded with a token gift/ sweet/fruit, etc.

RESPONDING TO UNACCEPTABLE BEHAVIOUR

The most important thing to remember when responding to unwanted behaviour is to:

- remain calm;
- handle the situation in a controlled manner.

CHILD'S NAME	STARS
Sam	★ ★ ★ ★ ★
David	★ ★ ★ ★ ★ ★ ★
Catherine	★ ★ ★ ★ ★
Isobel	★ ★ ★ ★ ★ ★ ★ ★ ★ ★ ★
Rebecca	★ ★ ★ ★ ★ ★ ★ ★ ★
Daisy	★ ★ ★ ★ ★ ★ ★ ★ ★ ★ ★
Alistair	★ ★ ★ ★ ★ ★
Juliette	★ ★ ★ ★ ★
Michael	★ ★ ★ ★ ★

Fig. 7. Example reward chart.

Never:

♦ shout or lose your temper;
♦ use physical punishment.

The method you choose to respond to unacceptable behaviour must be in keeping with the nature of the behaviour and appropriate to the child's age, stage of development and needs. By being aware of the factors which can trigger undesirable behaviour we can, where possible, eliminate many of the potential problems and we can at least try to understand those we cannot prevent. It will be much easier to respond to a child's unwanted behaviour if you are armed with an understanding of the circumstances and factors which have provoked the negative behaviour.

By responding to the situation in a calm manner you will show the children that *you* are in control, not them, and that negotiation is a more suitable option for diffusing the problem rather than shouting or violence.

The best way to deal with unwanted behaviour is to use positive, preventative strategies. By anticipating potential sources of danger or conflict and eliminating them, together with ensuring that children are well supervised and have interesting activities, you will be well on the way to creating a positive environment for children to thrive in. However, one thing is certain – children are not angels! They will all play up at some time and resort to some type of unwanted behaviour periodically. Figure 8 shows several ways you can intervene should a child behave inappropriately.

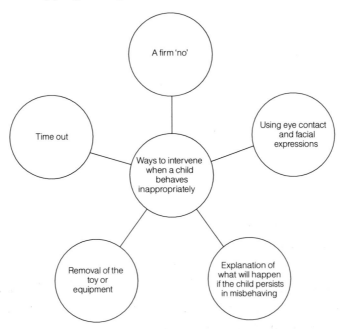

Fig. 8. Ways to intervene when a child behaves inappropriately.

Let us now look at these methods in more detail:

A firm 'NO'

Most children will respond well to this verbal expression and will usually understand its meaning from a very early age. For this command to work well though, it must be used sparingly. Saying 'no' to a child continually will result in frustration and testing of the boundaries. They will begin to think, 'Well, what *can* I do?' When you have told a child 'no', it is important that you explain why they are not allowed to do it and that you mean what you say. Never allow children to continue showing unacceptable behaviour or persuade you to change your mind. Saying 'no' coupled with the appropriate tone of voice and facial expression can be very effective.

TIP

Always mean what you say. A child must learn to understand that when you say 'no' it means 'no' and that you are not open to negotiation or persuasion.

Using eye contact and facial expressions

Sometimes a child who is aware of what is expected of them may test and try to overstep the boundaries. In these cases quite often a simple look is sufficient to let them know that their behaviour is unacceptable. Eye contact should be used with the appropriate facial expression, i.e. a look of disapproval.

Explanation of what will happen if the child persists

Children should always be made aware of the consequences of their actions. Explaining the consequences underlines the importance of the rules and sets clear boundaries. Never make idle threats. If you have warned a child of a consequence and they continue to show unacceptable behaviour, then it is paramount that you carry out the sanction you have imposed. By threatening sanctions that are unjustified or cannot be carried through you will undermine your own authority and confuse the child.

Removal of the toy or equipment

This should only be used as a last resort. Children should be allowed to rectify their behaviour initially, through compromise and warnings, before the toy or equipment is removed. By removing a toy or equipment *before* giving the child the opportunity to rectify their behaviour you will have taught them nothing. They will not know why you have taken the object away from them and will probably move on to another toy and continue with the same unwanted behaviour.

For example, if a child throws a toy across the room and you refuse to allow them to have it back, the child will simply pick up another toy and do the same thing. How are you going to solve this problem? Will you take away *all* the toys? You should say 'no' firmly, initially coupled with an expression of disapproval. If the behaviour persists, and the child is old enough to understand, then an explanation should be given as to why it is not acceptable to throw toys indoors. For example, the toy may hit someone and cause injury, it may break something, or the toy itself may be damaged. If you remove a toy or equipment from a child because they are displaying unacceptable behaviour and refuse to cooperate, it is a good idea to find the child something else to do to prevent them from creating another inappropriate situation elsewhere. If appropriate, try offering the child the opportunity of going outdoors to throw a ball as an alternative to throwing a toy indoors.

Time out

Time out is *not* the same as isolation. Isolating a child is not an effective method of behaviour management, and childminders should never put a child into a room and leave them alone. Time out is similar to removing toys and equipment in that it deprives the child of something they want. Time out allows both the child and the adult to calm down and take control of themselves. This method of behaviour management is particularly effective for more serious misdemeanours such as destructiveness, violence, swearing, rudeness, etc. A few minutes 'time out' should be long enough to diffuse the situation.

Time out is more appropriate for older children who will respond more effectively to being removed from a situation they are having difficulty with.

Time out should never be coupled with using a 'naughty chair' or 'naughty corner'. These are forms of humiliation and they will not help to calm a child down but will merely encourage anger and resentment. Time out is not a punishment, it is a way of getting a child to calm down and to step back from the problem. Offer reassurance and sympathy when talking to the child and remember that emotions are very powerful and are often difficult for a child to control.

IGNORING UNACCEPTABLE BEHAVIOUR

Whenever possible ignore a child who is exhibiting unacceptable behaviour. They are usually acting this way to gain attention and the best thing you can do is to refuse them the attention they are seeking whilst they are misbehaving. By giving a badly behaved child your attention you have effectively given them their own way. The attention they receive may not necessarily be desirable, but it is attention nonetheless. If possible, walk away from the child or busy yourself with a task which means you are taking no notice of what the child is doing. If a child sees that their unacceptable behaviour is having no affect on you they will quickly tire and move onto something else. A child who is acting disruptively for example is usually doing so for a reaction. He may be looking to shock, annoy, upset or anger you. By ignoring this behaviour you are refusing to allow him control over the situation and he will quickly realise that his efforts are in vain.

Obviously there are times when ignoring the behaviour or walking away from the child will not be an option; if, for example, their behaviour poses a danger to themselves or someone else, or if you are in a public place at the time. This is when distraction comes into its own.

Distraction
Distraction can be a very useful form of behaviour management when other methods fail. A child who is causing a scene because she wants a

toy that someone else is playing with can have her behaviour successfully managed by the use of distraction. Failure to get what she wants could result in a tantrum; however by distracting her and getting her interested in another toy, you may be able to diffuse the situation and avert the problem.

Play therapy

Play therapy is an ideal way for children to act out situations that cause anxiety and stress and which may lead to problems with behaviour. It provides a child with a way to release strong emotions in a safe environment and in a non-threatening way.

Play therapy can be used in a number of ways such as:

◆ Physical play – kicking a ball about outside or running around a playground are good ways of releasing pent up energy which could turn into anger and frustration.

◆ Play dough and clay are good for kneading when feelings of frustration are threatening to take over.

◆ Role play is good for expressing anxiety and fear which a child may experience before a hospital appointment or a change in schools, for example.

◆ Books are an excellent source of information about a huge range of topics including bereavement, visiting the dentist, dealing with a new baby, moving house, starting school, etc.

**SIX EFFECTIVE STEPS TO PROMOTE
POSITIVE BEHAVIOUR IN CHILDREN**

◆ Be consistent – mean what you say!
◆ Be a good role model – children copy what they see and hear.
◆ Use praise and rewards – children love to please.
◆ Ignore bad behaviour whenever possible.
◆ Use 'time out' to diffuse the situation.
◆ Apply sanctions whenever necessary.

TIP

Whatever strategy you choose, it is important to make children aware that it is their *behaviour* that you do not like and not the child themselves.

THE LAW AND SMACKING

For the purpose of caring for other people's children it is vital to understand that any childminder or nursery provision regulated by Ofsted is prohibited from using any form of physical punishment on a child. Physical punishment includes:

- smacking;
- shaking;
- pushing;
- kicking;
- rough handling in any way.

Childminders, nursery nurses, teachers, etc. are all bound by their regulations and must *never* resort to physical punishment.

Many parents, and indeed childcare practitioners, believe that giving a child a quick smack is an effective way of instantly getting a child to stop behaving in an unacceptable way. Others believe that smacking is completely unnecessary and sends out the wrong messages.

There have been many debates and discussions about the use of physical punishment on children and, in particular, the right to smack a child. The biggest problem is ascertaining what constitutes a 'smack'. What one person might consider a light tap may be seen as a sharp slap by another, and this is where the problems arise. In the past, childminders have been allowed to smack the children in their care with written permission from the parents. However problems might then arise about:

- the severity of the smack;
- the circumstances surrounding the smack;
- whether the child had been marked by the smack;

◆ whether the punishment was in keeping with parental wishes.

The simple way around these problems is to ban all types of physical punishment in a day-care setting. This was achieved for childminders when, on 4 May 2003 after years of campaigning by the National Childminding Association, the Government announced that child-minders in England would no longer be allowed to smack the children in their care. This new guidance came into effect for childminders in September 2003.

A new law came into force in January 2005 stating that any parent in England and Wales who smacks their child so hard that it leaves a mark may face up to five years in jail. This law was designed to allow parents to take a 'common sense' approach to discipline. The law states that mild smacking is allowed as reasonable chastisement.

Although Britain signed the United Nations Convention of the Rights of the Child more than 15 years ago it has still failed to impose a total ban against smacking.

The new law throws open many questions such as:

1. How can the law be enforced?

2. Will the law tempt parents to smack their children on parts of the body where marks are less visible which are equally or more damaging, such as on the head?

3. How will the law protect children of different races whose skin may not show markings in the same way as a child with white skin?

4. How big does the mark have to be for the smack to be deemed illegal?

5. How long does the mark have to be visible for after the smack has been administered?

The law states that any smack which leaves a child with a bruise, graze, scratch, cut or swelling will not be permitted.

Laws aside, what we should really be concentrating on is whether or not smacking is necessary. It may be argued that a child who is smacked by an adult learns that it is acceptable for a bigger person to inflict pain and suffering on a smaller person, and that violence is acceptable. Smacking is a form of aggressive behaviour and an adult smacking a child gives the message that it is acceptable to resort to this type of aggression. Although smacking may prevent a child from acting in a certain way, it does not actually teach them how to resolve problems or conflicts in a peaceful way.

Many European countries have already brought a law into force completely banning anyone, including parents, from smacking children, and there are many people in this country who think a total ban on smacking is the only answer.

7

Child Development

Although we often refer to the growth and development of the 'average' child there is, in fact, no such thing. Every child is unique with their own traits and characteristics which will affect their development from the moment they are conceived throughout their lives. As a childminder, what you must be aware of is that all babies and children are *whole* human beings, and whilst we may, from time to time, look at various aspects of their growth and development, it is the person as a whole which we should be particularly concerned with.

Children's development is affected by many different influences, for example where they live and the people they meet, and it is important for childminders to understand how and why children grow and develop in the way that they do. You will need to be aware of the way in which children grow and develop in order to plan and provide for their needs.

MILESTONES IN GROWTH AND DEVELOPMENT

Child development is the growth of babies through childhood. Children will develop as they grow. All children will go through the same stages of development, albeit at differing speeds. Whilst some children can walk unaided and confidently at 12 months, others may take a further six months or more to reach this stage. What is clear, however, is that each child must reach a certain degree of development in one stage before they can progress onto another. For example a child will learn to sit before they can stand, stand before they can walk and walk before they can run. Although most of this information seems logical it is important that you understand and recognise the clearly defined stages of child development when carrying out your childminding duties.

Understanding the milestones

There are several reasons why it is important for childminders to understand these 'milestones' in a child's life and Figure 9 shows some of these reasons.

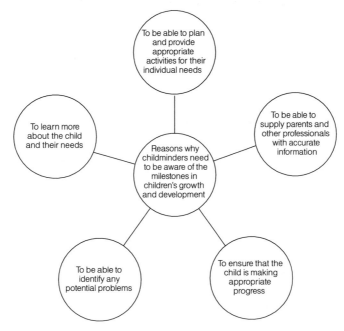

Fig. 9. Reasons to be aware of the milestones
in children's growth and development.

Let us now look at these points in more detail.

1. To be able to plan and provide appropriate activities for their individual needs

It is necessary for childminders to be aware of the milestones achieved by each child they are caring for in order to plan activities suited to their individual stage of growth and development. There would be little point in planning a complex painting activity, for example, if the child it was aimed at had not mastered fine motor skills and found handling a paintbrush difficult.

2. To be able to supply parents and other professionals with accurate information

As a childminder you will be expected to tell parents what their child has been doing with you during the day. By sharing information of this kind with them you will be involving them in the day-to-day activities enjoyed in your setting and building up a friendship based on trust. From time to time it may be necessary to share information about a child with other professionals, with the parents' consent, and it is absolutely crucial that the information you supply is accurate and up to date.

3. To ensure that the child is making appropriate progress
It is essential that childminders know what stage of growth and development the children in their care are at in order to ascertain whether they are making sufficient progress. It is a good idea to assess each child when they start in your setting and review your assessments periodically to help you to decide whether they are making suitable progress.

4. To be able to identify any potential problems
By assessing the children in your care you will be able to identify any areas for concern. You may, after assessing the child, find they have problems in certain areas of their development which requires additional help and support.

5. To learn more about the child and their needs
The more information you can gain about a child the better equipped you will be to care for them and provide for their needs. By being aware of each child's developmental stage, you can choose appropriate activities and you will know when to extend these activities as the child develops and becomes more confident.

AREAS OF GROWTH AND DEVELOPMENT

Different terms are often used for the study of children's growth and development. The two most common terms are **SPICE** and **PILES**. Both of these acronyms point to the different areas of growth and development.

SPICE

S **S**ocial

P **P**hysical

I **I**ntellectual

C **C**ommunication

E **E**motional

PILES

P **P**hysical

I **I**ntellectual

L **L**anguage

E **E**motional

S **S**ocial

Whichever method you use to remember the aspects of a child's development is not really relevant. What is relevant, however, is that you understand the importance of the child's development in *all* of these areas.

We can extend the areas of development into *The Seven C's*. These seven areas are of great importance for a child's development:

1. Confidence
2. Co-ordination
3. Communication
4. Concentration
5. Co-operation
6. Competence
7. Creativity

The holistic approach

Although it is important to be aware of all of the areas of growth and development it is equally important to remember that a child grows and develops not in separate *areas* but as a whole. When we talk about child development as a whole we refer to the *holistic approach*. By looking at the growth and development of a child as a whole we are much better equipped to understand *why* a child behaves in a certain way and the reasons behind the things they do.

For example, a child who is asked to help to clear away the toys before story time may ignore the request for a number of reasons:

1. They may not have understood the request.
2. They may be absorbed in an activity and simply didn't hear the request.
3. They may have a hearing problem.
4. They may be seeking attention.
5. They may simply not want to tidy up!

By looking at the child as a 'whole' and taking the holistic approach, we are able to work out the variety of reasons for the child's behaviour.

Although all children grow and develop at different rates we will now look at the areas of growth and development in three monthly intervals over a child's first year of life. Remember that these intervals are a *rough* guide as all children are unique and no two babies will grow and develop at exactly the same rate.

BIRTH TO ONE YEAR

Birth to three months
In the first three months of their lives, most babies will spend their time with their parents who are likely to be on leave from work. It is unlikely that as a childminder you will be caring for a baby younger than 12 weeks. Newborn babies are completely dependent on their carers to provide for them. They are unable to do even the smallest task for themselves and as such it is important that if you are caring for a newborn that you understand their needs and provide for them.

Babies grow and develop very quickly, particularly in their first year of life. They will go from being defenceless individuals to being able to recognise people and objects, sit up, clap hands, wave and possibly even walk before they reach their first birthday.

Newborn babies, although totally dependent on others, are actually aware of the things around them. They will already have reflexes which will enable them to react to certain things such as:

- human contact;
- bright lights;
- sudden movement;
- loud noises.

Before a baby has reached one month they will be able to recognise the sound of their main carer's voice and be able to distinguish some familiar sounds.

Working on the *Piles* theory, 'normative measurements' of a child's growth and development may look something like those on pages 100–105.

FACTORS WHICH MAY AFFECT A CHILD'S GROWTH AND DEVELOPMENT

There are many factors which may affect a child's growth and development. Some of these factors may be temporary and some permanent. These factors are numerous but may range from a cold which results in a temporary loss of hearing to an illness such as cystic fibrosis which will affect the child's growth and development permanently.

Studies have divided the factors which affect growth and development into three categories:

- Antenatal: the time from conception to birth;
- Perinatal: the actual time of the birth;
- Postnatal: the time after the birth.

Antenatal: At the time of conception many factors may influence and affect the growth and development of the child. Things such as the mother's diet, whether she smokes and consumes alcohol and whether she is fit and healthy all contribute to the growth and development of the child.

Birth to three months

Physical	Intellectual	Language	Emotional	Social
The baby lies on their back.	Feels pain.	Babies respond to various situations by either crying, gurgling or cooing.	Babies first start to smile at around five to six weeks.	Babies of this age enjoy feeding and being in close contact with their carer.
Head falls forward and back curves.	Turns towards sounds, listens to voices.	They can recognise familiar voices and will turn to look for the sound.	By the age of eight to twelve weeks a baby will recognise the face and voice of their main carer.	A crying baby may stop being distressed when they hear, see or feel their main carer.
Towards the end of this stage the baby can lift the head and kick vigorously.	Can 'root' and will turn towards the smell of the breast.	They will quieten when picked up and will cry when hungry, tired or uncomfortable.		Babies of this age often enjoy intimate caring routines such as cuddles and bathtime.
The baby recognises bright lights and shiny objects.	Babies can focus on objects up to a few inches away.			
Will react to loud noises and recognise their main carer's face.	Babies enjoy imitating facial expressions and can make eye contact at this age.			
Towards the end of this stage the baby can watch hands and play with fingers and rattles.				

Three to six months

Physical	Intellectual	Language	Emotional	Social
The baby is now likely to be able to grasp and switch objects from one hand to the other.	Babies have the ability to reach for objects. They like bright colours and interesting things to keep them stimulated.	Babies of this age can recognise sounds and as they listen they try to imitate the sounds they hear.	By the age of five months a baby has learned that they have only one mother.	Babies of this age are very interested in what is going on around them.
Attempts to put objects in the mouth.	Co-ordination is improving.	Babies are able to laugh and show signs of pleasure.	Babies of this age show trust and security and they enjoy being in contact with others and receiving attention from them.	
Has good head control.				

Six to nine months

Physical	Intellectual	Language	Emotional	Social
A baby of this age can now usually roll from front to back.	The baby is now needing more complex and interesting things to keep them amused. They enjoy games of peek-a-boo and are fascinated watching brightly moving objects.	Babies continue to try to imitate the sounds they hear and will constantly babble using sounds like 'ah' and 'ee'.	May begin to become distressed if the mother leaves the baby's sight.	May begin to feed themselves with fingers.
May attempt to crawl.			Become aware of people they do not know.	Enjoys laughing with others.
Grasps feet.				

Nine to twelve months

Physical	Intellectual	Language	Emotional	Social
By this age the child will probably be mobile. This could mean either shuffling, crawling or even walking.	At this stage of a child's development they will begin to remember things and build on memory.	The child may be able to respond to simple instructions such as 'kiss mummy'.	Enjoys being with familiar people.	Enjoys playing alone and can manage this for lengthy periods of time.
The child will be able to sit unaided.	They will become adept at imitating others including their actions, sounds and moods.	Babble becomes expressive and continual.	Begins to show preferences.	Enjoys music and nursery rhymes.
Pincer movement is well developed and the child should be able to reach and grasp objects.	The child will be able to wave goodbye and clap hands.	May be able to imitate sounds of animals such as 'baa', 'moo', etc.	Continues to enjoy games such as 'peek-a-boo' and becomes more confident clapping hands and waving goodbye.	
The child will be able to throw toys and manage to feed themselves with finger foods.				

ONE TO EIGHT YEARS

One year

Physical	Intellectual	Language	Emotional	Social
By the age of one year there is a good chance that the baby may be mobile, either by crawling or walking. The baby can probably manage to climb stairs under supervision but will find it difficult to maintain balance. They will probably be able to kneel without support and get to their feet using objects/furniture to help them.	Although children of this age cannot see things from different points of view they are able to focus on one aspect of a situation at a time. They begin to understand that people think in different ways and have different likes and dislikes.	Children of this age begin to talk. They will use basic sounds and simple words.	Children of this age become aware when others are happy, sad or distressed and will often react accordingly. For example they may cry when someone is hurt although they themselves are not actually feeling the pain.	By the time a child reaches the age of one year they have often developed a sense of identity which will progress throughout the following months. They will enjoy being mobile and relish the idea of discovering things for themselves.

Two years

Physical	Intellectual	Language	Emotional	Social
By the age of two years the child will be very mobile, being able to run and climb. They should be able to negotiate steps and stairs with ease although this may be with two feet at a time rather than with alternate feet. Although not able to catch a ball yet, they should be confident at kicking one.	By now the child will probably have discovered 'pretend play' and will enjoy talking to themselves whilst playing in this way. They may enjoy music and making sound from instruments.	By the time the child reaches the age of two years it is thought that their vocabulary is extended to around 50 words although they may understand many more. Children's speech by the age of two is rapidly expanding and they become increasingly confident sharing songs and conversation.	The child's sense of identity progresses rapidly at the age of two years. Memory increases.	At the age of two children are becoming more and more confident and are eager to do things for themselves such as getting dressed and helping with simple tasks.

Three years

Physical	Intellectual	Language	Emotional	Social
By now the child can confidently jump from low heights, walk backwards and sideways, stand and walk on tip toe and balance on one foot.	The child can control a pencil and will often enjoy painting. They may be able to use scissors to cut paper.	By now a child's language has progressed rapidly and they can communicate very well using plurals, tenses and sentences.	The child has now become aware of their feelings and may often describe how they are feeling.	By now the child is capable of making friends.
They should be able to negotiate stairs one foot at a time and may be able to ride a tricycle.	Pretend play continues and develops.	At the age of three years children love to talk and may ask questions incessantly. They enjoy listening to stories and repetition is not unusual as by now the child will have his or her favourite story which they may request over and over again.	Children of this age become aware of the gender differences.	They understand how to negotiate and take turns although they may quarrel and resort to tantrums when they do not get their own way.
			Many children of this age become easily afraid of the unknown or things they are unsure of such as the dark, spiders, etc.	
		Frustration is common at this age as often their thinking can over take their ability to express themselves verbally.	Children can now dress themselves and go to the toilet independently.	

Four years

Physical	Intellectual	Language	Emotional	Social
By now the child can do many things physically: balance and walk along a straight line, catch, kick, throw and bounce a ball, climb, and run up and down steps one foot at a time.	Children of the age of four can draw recognisable objects. For example, a person will consist of a body, two arms, two legs and a head. They can thread small beads on a string. Memory is developing fast and the child can think back and look forward.	This is the age when children become very inquisitive and often ask questions. Words such as why, how, when and if are frequently used.	The emotional stage of a four year-old child is very much the same as that of a three year-old. They may still be afraid of the unknown. Their imagination runs riot at this age and they are capable of imagining a wide variety of things.	A four year-old child is increasingly interested in making friends and enjoys socialising with others.

Five years

Physical	Intellectual	Language	Emotional	Social
The child's ability to do physical things has increased greatly by the age of five years and they can now confidently use a variety of equipment, play ball games, skip and hop. Their balance is good and they are able to move to music.	By the age of five children are beginning to learn the concepts of literacy and numeracy and can confidently count. They can now differentiate between real and pretend and are interested in everything around them. Fine motor skills are well developed. Drawings begin to resemble the objects intended.	Children at the age of five years are confident speakers and are very adept at understanding the meaning of numerous words. Language, at this age, is used in a creative fashion.	Children of this age are capable of hiding their feelings and controlling their emotions. They are aware of how others may be feeling.	At the age of five years, children are very aware of their gender and are familiar with their own culture. They enjoy being with others and having friends. Sharing and turn taking is more widely practised. They are beginning to work out what is right and wrong.

Six to eight years

Physical	Intellectual	Language	Emotional	Social
Between the ages of six and eight years a child's physical development increases to the stage where they can confidently jump heights and ride a two-wheel bicycle.	By now the child can draw confidently and write letters and numbers.	Language becomes more complex and the use of different words widens.	Quarrels begin to surface more frequently at this age when children become increasingly demanding and stubborn.	Children of this age may forge friendships with one 'special' person.
Their balance has improved greatly and their agility increased.	Reading and mathematical skills are developing and they will be able to write independently.	The child will be able to describe objects accurately and give opposite meanings.	Mood changes begin to surface.	The child may prefer to spend increasing amounts of time alone.
			Importance is put on peer approval and the emphasis to succeed becomes apparent.	Children between the ages of six and eight years may become less sociable.

Perinatal: A baby who has gone full term before birth will be born between 38 and 40 weeks of pregnancy. A premature baby, on the other hand, may be born between 24 and 37 weeks and may well be under developed when born, depending on how premature they are. A premature baby is likely to be small and have a low birth weight and can have developmental delays. Other problems which may arise include feeding difficulties, breathing problems and a higher risk of infection.

Postnatal: One of the problems experienced by some babies at birth is the lack of oxygen during the actual birthing process. A baby who has been deprived of oxygen at birth is likely to suffer from a wide range of problems such as cerebral palsy and severe learning difficulties.

Below is a list of some of the more common factors which may affect a child's growth and development:

- diet;
- food allergies;
- health problems;
- accidents;
- culture;
- environment;
- loss or bereavement;
- separation or divorce of parents;
- lack of stimulation and appropriate toys;
- learning difficulties.

Let us now look at these factors in more detail.

Diet

A healthy, balanced diet is absolutely crucial for children. A child who is undernourished or who is not fed a balanced diet may well suffer from developmental delays. The correct food is an essential form of energy which encourages the child to grow and develop.

Childminders must *always* be in agreement with parents when providing meals for the children they are caring for. You should discuss preferences with the parents and ensure that factors such as culture, religion and medical reasons are taken into account. *Never* offer a child something which the parent has specifically asked you not to; you must respect their wishes at all times.

For a child's body to develop and grow at a normal pace it requires five important nutrients. These nutrients are:

1. **Proteins**: These are found in meat, fish, vegetables, dairy products and soya. Proteins encourage the body to grow and assist the healing process.

2. **Fats**: These are found in meat, fish, vegetable oils and dairy products. Fats provide the body with energy.

3. **Vitamins**: Vitamins can be found in many forms and are derived from fresh food products such as fruit and vegetables. Vitamins are essential for growth and development.

4. **Carbohydrates**: These are found in potatoes, bread, vegetables and bananas. Carbohydrates provide the body with energy.

5. **Minerals**: Minerals such as calcium and iron are essential for growth and development. Iron can be found in meat and some green vegetables whereas calcium is found in milk and other dairy products.

Food allergies

Food allergies are very common in children and can either affect them all of their lives or they can be short-lived and grown out of.

Allergies to some foods can be very serious and if you care caring for a child with, for example a nut allergy, it is vital that you ensure that they do not come into contact with this type of foodstuff. An allergy to nuts and shellfish can bring on an anaphylactic shock which results in breathing difficulties due to the airways swelling up. Anaphylactic shocks can be fatal.

Diabetes, asthma and eczema are also very common in children. Diabetes can, once again, be fatal and it is important that diabetic children eat well balanced diets and avoid sugar. Glucose must be given if the sugar levels drop too low to avoid the child going into a seizure or coma.

Asthma and eczema have been known to be aggravated by some foods, particularly dairy products. Additives such as tartrazine which is found in fizzy drinks and sweets may lead to hyperactivity and the inability to concentrate.

Health problems

As a childminder you will need to ascertain whether the children you are caring for are suffering from any health problems which may affect the child when they are with you. The issues surrounding health are numerous and whilst some may be short-lived such as chicken pox, colds and ear infections, others may be more serious such as cystic fibrosis or coeliac disease.

Accidents

Keeping children safe and ensuring that the premises are suitable for young children should be a priority for all childminders. However, sometimes even the most vigilant childminder or parent cannot prevent an accident from happening. A child who has been involved in a serious accident will of course suffer from some kind of developmental delay if they have been affected in the way they move, walk, talk, etc. Language may also be affected if the child has suffered trauma and they may become clingy, withdrawn and frightened. Quite often, depending on the nature of the accident, developmental delays can be rectified and with the appropriate care and understanding the child can make a full recovery.

Culture

As a childminder it is paramount that you respect the culture of all the children in your care and that you treat each child as an individual and with respect. If the traditions followed by the family are different from your own and you do not understand them then it is very important that you seek the parents' advice. Most parents will be happy to talk to you and offer help where necessary. You will need to be a positive role model for the children and encourage them to learn about cultures other than their own.

Environment

A child's environment and the way they are brought up can have a huge affect on all aspects of their growth and development. Poor housing and lack of money can affect a child's health as often the amount and quality of food provided for them is poor, and they may not have sufficient heating and water.

Loss or bereavement

Children often find it difficult to put things into perspective and may view the loss of a favourite toy on the same level as the death of a close relative. Loss and bereavement can be very traumatic for children who will all react differently to this type of situation. Some will be openly traumatised whilst others may try to hide their feelings.

Separation or divorce of parents

Individual children will react differently to the separation or divorce of their parents. Much will depend on the child's age and their ability to understand what is happening. Some children may suffer both emotionally and socially as a result of their parents' relationship break-up and may become anxious and withdrawn; others may cope very well and appear to be unaffected by the changes. As a childminder it is important that you are never seen to apportion blame or side with either parent. Of course it may be possible that you are not privy to the goings on in the family circumstances and the parents may choose only to inform you of the break down of the relationship after the event, so it is vital that you are conscious of any changes in a child's usual behaviour and that you tread carefully and sensitively. Never probe or ask questions, simply offer support and understanding when necessary.

Lack of stimulation and appropriate toys

All children enjoy exploring and discovering things for themselves. They should be allowed to investigate the world around them in order to develop their skills. It is absolutely essential that children are provided with activities and toys which will stimulate them and which are appropriate to their stage of development. Progress will falter if children are not stimulated appropriately.

Learning difficulties

Learning difficulties are many and varied, and they can affect all areas of children's growth and development. If you have agreed to care for a child who has obvious learning difficulties then you will, of course, discuss any issues with the child's parents and work out a suitable strategy. However there may be times, as the child develops, when you notice that a child in your care is having difficulty with something which has not already been identified. In cases such as this you will need to discuss your concerns, *sympathetically*, with the parents and decide together what course of action should be taken.

8

Suitable Activities for Children

PLANNING APPROPRIATELY

There is little point in planning and preparing activities for children if you do not take into account their age and stage of development. A badly planned activity which is either too easy or too difficult for the child it is intended for is just as bad as no activity at all.

Activities which are too easy will result in boredom and lack of attention. The child will quickly tire and become fidgety, or will wander off to find something more interesting to occupy themselves with. Activities which are too difficult will also result in lack of concentration and may even have the affect of reducing the child's self-esteem as they may feel they have failed.

It is therefore vital that you consider closely the children you are caring for before deciding on which activities to provide. Think about the following aspects:

- The age of the child.
- The stage of the child's development (some children are more advanced than others even though they are the same age).
- The child's preferences.
- The concentration capacity of the child. Some children at the age of three years, for example, may happily sit and do a jigsaw whilst others of the same age cannot sit for more than a few minutes, preferring to take part in more 'active' pastimes.

By taking the above factors into account for each child, you should be able to assess quickly which activities are suitable for which child. Once you have ascertained this you can start to plan your activities and provide for each child's stage of development.

Some childminders find it easier to plan their activities around a theme, and this works well providing you are not too focused on the theme and forget to make time for spontaneous play. Allowing children the freedom of choice is essential, and if you have planned a particular activity and the children do not appear interested in it, do not despair, allow them time to play in the sand or with the train set and come back to the 'planned' activity later. Forcing young children to sit and take part in something if they are not happy doing so will not achieve anything. They will be reluctant to do what is expected of them and may even rush through the planned activity, gaining little from the experience, simply to return to their preferred play.

BIRTH TO 12 MONTHS

Suitable activities to promote development at this stage in a baby's life include:

◆ **Talking**. It is very important that the main carers in a young baby's life talk to them. Whilst talking to the baby look directly at them and position your face near to theirs as initially they are unable to focus beyond a few inches.

◆ **Brightly coloured objects and musical mobiles**. Young babies will respond to light and sounds.

◆ Lots of 'first toys' such as:
   – rattles;
   – scraps of fabric with different textures;
   – solid objects such as balls;
   – silver foil;
   – shiny objects such as a mirror;
   – measuring spoons;
   – stacking plastic beakers.

Many objects can be home-made providing the materials you use are clean and safe. Always supervise a young baby when they are playing with toys, and make sure that objects such as mobiles hung over a cot are out of the baby's reach so that they cannot pull themselves up or become entangled in them.

◆ **A treasure basket**: This is an excellent source of entertainment for a young child and will provide them with lots of opportunities to stimulate the five senses. Treasure baskets can be successfully used once the baby can sit up. Include about 15 to 20 objects made of natural materials, carefully chosen for their texture and shape. The items should be clean and perishable objects replaced regularly. Always make sure that the objects you choose are appropriate for the child's age and avoid small items which can be inserted in the nose or ears or which may pose a choking hazard. Items you may like to consider for a treasure basket include:
  – a small mirror
  – a clean, dry fir cone
  – a pumice stone
  – a small natural sponge
  – a bunch of keys
  – a large shell
  – an orange
  – a clothes' peg
  – a ball of crumpled tissue paper
  – a piece of foil
  – a large pebble.

Although young babies are unable to take part in games and planned activities which are often enjoyed by older children, they do enjoy having things to look at, listen to, hold and feel, and it is these aspects you should be looking to build on and develop. The senses should be stimulated and you will find that young babies are fascinated by a variety of miscellaneous objects which are found in most houses such as:

◆ A ball of string.
◆ A plastic bottle.

- Clean, empty boxes of various shapes and sizes.
- Balls of various sizes – do not offer anything smaller than a tennis ball.
- Parcels: try putting a rattle in a paper bag or loosely wrapping it in paper for the baby to unwrap.
- Books – avoid books with paper pages as these will invariably get eaten or torn. There are many board books on the market which have bright pictures to appeal to young babies. Turning the pages holds endless fascination for children of this age.
- Kitchen roll tubes.
- A ladle.
- A wooden spoon.

The list is endless and simply by looking around your own home you will discover lots of items which will fascinate a young baby.

Playing 'finger' games, clapping and waving are enjoyed by most babies of this age. Making the time to enjoy everyday opportunities such as changing nappies and bath time will all encourage the child's development. Allow extra time for the baby to kick and splash about in the water, for example, to stretch and exercise their arms and legs.

As the child gets older, try encouraging movement and crawling by placing familiar objects slightly out of their reach so that they have to move towards them.

> **TIP**
>
> Remember it is not always necessary to purchase toys to stimulate small babies and young children. Often home-made resources will hold endless fascination and stimulate a child's senses equally as well as an expensive shop bought toy. Use your imagination and experiment!

ONE TO TWO YEARS

Between the ages of one and two years children are really beginning to explore their surroundings and are keen to experiment. They enjoy putting things in different types of containers and taking things out.

They are beginning to take control of their co-ordination and can sit unaided to enjoy many activities. As children are beginning to stand and walk, push-a-long toys and other equipment which assist balance and walking can be used. I would, however, always deter childminders from using baby walkers as these can be very dangerous and have in fact been known to hinder rather than aid a child's ability to walk.

Suitable activities for children of this age include:

♦ Sand and water play: always supervise children when they are playing in or around water.

♦ Messy activities such as finger painting. Experiment with shaving foam, flour and water mixtures, etc.

♦ Mark-making and colouring with a variety of materials can be introduced. Provide chunky crayons, thick paint brushes and large pieces of paper.

♦ Expand on the idea of the treasure basket which we looked at earlier in this chapter, adding items such as baking tins, larger boxes, lengths of tube, corks, etc.

♦ Large beads and lengths of cord to encourage the child to thread and lace.

TWO TO FOUR YEARS

Children of this age like to play with a variety of toys and equipment and enjoy pretend play in addition to creative play. Provide items such as:

♦ Dressing-up clothes.

♦ Dolls and soft toys.

♦ Toys which mirror everyday life such as cooking equipment, tea sets, sweeping brushes, pretend iron and ironing board.

♦ Play dough.

- Creative materials such as paints and crayons. Offer a variety of equipment for the children to experiment with such as different sized brushes, sponges, scrapers, string, and textured cards and papers.

- Baking: children love to bake. Seek out simple, no-cook recipes for the very young such as chocolate krispie buns, jellies or refrigerator cakes, and progress to buns and cakes as the children get older. Decorating plain buns and biscuits with icing sugar and cake decorations is another enjoyable activity for children of this age group.

- Sand and water play: always supervise children near water.

- Gardening: offer opportunities to explore the garden and allow the children the chance to plant seeds, water and care for them, and then watch and record the plants as they grow. This encourages early science and children are fascinated by the changes. Sunflower seeds are particularly good as they grow quickly and need little care other than watering.

- Puzzles.

- Construction toys.

- Books.

- Games: simple games such as snakes and ladders can be played with four year-olds and games of animal snap can be introduced to younger children.

- Objects to 'sort': children between the ages of two and four love to sort things out. They will enjoy grouping items together and sorting them into piles of similar colours, shapes and sizes. Provide duplo bricks, stickle bricks, boxes and other containers in order for them to enjoy this activity which introduces early mathematical concepts.

Children between the ages of two and four are developing fast and learning quickly. They are interested in everything around them and are eager for new experiences. It is important that childminders, who may be caring for more than one child between the ages of two and four, remember that sharing and taking turns is still very much a part of the child's learning process at this developmental stage. You may need to provide lots of resources for this age group to avoid unnecessary disputes between the children. Try purchasing several dolls for example and provide a selection of dressing-up clothes and role play items.

FOUR TO FIVE YEARS

Children between the ages of four and five are often boisterous and energetic. They are enjoying discovering the world around them and are eager to make progress and develop. Children of this age group will enjoy:

♦ Reading. Make sure you have a good range of books to suit the interests of all the children in your care. Consider joining your local library, if you have not already done so, as this is an excellent way of providing a variety of reading material. Take the children with you when you visit the library and allow them to choose books which are of interest to them. Library visits can be a good learning experience.

♦ Helping with the everyday tasks you need to carry out. Allow the children to set the table and clear up after meals. Let them prepare simple snacks, sort the clean washing or put away the shopping. You will be amazed at the many ways that all of these tasks help and support a child's learning. For example, they will be encouraged to use mathematics when setting the table by having to count how many people will be eating the meal and how many knives, forks and spoons will be needed. Allowing the children the chance to put away the shopping encourages them to be aware of food stuffs and how they are stored and gives them the opportunity to feel the weights and sizes of various packages.

Starting school

Usually children in this age group are starting school for the first time. It is important to remember that all children will deal with the transition into school differently. Sometimes even the most confident of children, whom you would least expect to feel out of their depth, may feel vulnerable and anxious at the prospect of entering a whole new world. Plenty of patience and encouragement is usually all that is needed to ease children into their first year of schooling.

Always remember that children who have just started school may well be very tired at the end of their day, and may find the routine exhausting for some time. Allow them to relax in any way they wish after school and do not push or over stimulate them with activities if they are not interested. Make sure the child is aware of the activities on offer but allow them to decide what, if anything, they wish to do. Some children may be tired and cross, and you will need to bear this in mind and, if necessary, adjust your routine accordingly.

Stories are a particularly good way for children to wind down after a busy day and introducing time to read to the children will be both beneficial and enjoyable. As the children become older and more adept at reading themselves you can incorporate time for them to read to you in the routine.

SCHOOL-AGED CHILDREN

Children who have been at school for some time will be familiar with their routine and will no longer be exhausted after a day in the classroom, making it possible for them to enjoy activities outside of school. Some children may enrol in classes after school such as sport, music, drama or art, while others prefer to leave at the end of lessons.

Although it is often thought that the older a child becomes the more at ease with themselves they appear and the more confident they grow, this is not always the case. For example, many six year-olds are not as emotionally stable as five year-olds as they become more and more self conscious. They can become victims of embarrassment and shyness, and many become rebellious and self-centred. When asked to describe their six year-olds, many parents will use conflicting words such as co-operative and rebellious, loving and selfish. This is because at this age the child is learning to explore their emotions and experiment with boundaries.

As the child gets older and enters their seventh and eighth years they are becoming more and more independent, however they still place a great deal of weight on the opinions of their peers, teachers, older children and carers. It is absolutely vital that you are a good role model at all times for children but never more so than at this impressionable age when children often find failure frustrating and need constant praise and encouragement to acknowledge their efforts and achievements.

Think about providing the following:

◆ Activities and materials to stretch concentration levels, such as more complex construction sets or jigsaw puzzles with a large number of small pieces.

◆ Electronic games which can be played at different levels.

◆ Musical instruments.

◆ Outdoor play suitable to their age such as games of rounders, cricket or football, where they can learn how to play in teams and understand the rules of the games.

◆ Consider taking the children on appropriate outings during school holidays which will be both interesting and educational, such as a visit to a museum or specially organised events.

◆ Introduce more complex recipes to enable the children to take part in baking and cooking activities.

◆ Consider buying a small pet for the children to be responsible for whilst they are at your house. A goldfish, rabbit or guinea pig would be an ideal way of introducing the children to the responsibilities of caring for an animal and each child should be given a specific role to play in the pet's upkeep, for example feeding, grooming, cleaning out, etc. Of course you must bear in mind that you will have overall responsibility for the pet, particularly at weekends and during holidays, so bear this in mind before committing yourself.

◆ Introduce creative activities such as sewing and making jewellery. Most children of this age will enjoy taking part in activities which result in a finished product which they can take home and keep, and they will take pride in the work they produce.

When caring for children before and after school it is very important that you remember that they may not wish to take part in all of the activities on offer and they should be allowed to choose for themselves.

Aim to provide a quiet area where the children can complete homework tasks or sit quietly to read. Avoid being too strict when it comes to watching television and allow them time to enjoy their favourite programmes after school. Bear in mind that they will have been busy working in the classroom all day and will need to wind down and relax afterwards.

COMBINING THE CARE OF CHILDREN OF DIFFERENT AGES

The challenges

One of the most difficult things for a childminder to achieve is combining the care of children of different ages successfully. Babies can be very demanding and strict sleep and feed patterns need to be followed. Toddlers are by nature very inquisitive and will, given the chance, get themselves into all sorts of scrapes if not supervised adequately. Children who have just started school may lack confidence, be exhausted or simply unhappy in their change in routine and need lots of attention and encouragement. Older children may easily become bored and require constant stimulation. Juggling all of these needs is not easy. However it is possible and, furthermore, it is essential if you are to provide the type of childcare the children require and do justice to yourself and your business.

Nobody said that childminding was an easy profession to be in and the demands on your time are exceptional in this type of work. However, the rewards of working with young children are high and you will reap the benefits of careful planning when the children are healthy, happy and well adjusted.

Juggling different children's needs

Childminding is all about partnerships. You must work closely with the parents and the children to provide for their needs and to ensure that *all* the children in your care are happy. There is no excuse for a childminder to ignore an older child in order to care for a younger one and school-aged children should not be made to 'fend for themselves' whilst you look after a baby.

It is essential that all the children feel welcome and valued, and the only way to ensure this is to make time for them. Make sure you show an interest in what they have to say and be genuinely concerned for their welfare. Of course there may be times when you have to ask them to wait until you have changed the baby's nappy or fed them a bottle before you can help with their homework but as long as you do help them with their homework in the end, having to wait a few minutes will be of no detriment. It is when you promise something and do not see it through that the child will start to feel unimportant and irrelevant.

Older children can, of course, be included in some of the routine work of caring for the younger ones and, in many cases, they will enjoy the responsibility. The tasks you allow them to carry out will depend on the child's age but you should never expect them to change a nappy, feed a baby or be responsible for a younger child's safety. This is *your* responsibility and *yours* alone.

How many children to take?

Although most childminders can care for three children under the age of five years, this does not mean that all childminders *must* care for this number of children. This is the maximum number and many child-minders may be quite happy to care for just one or two children under the age of five, particularly if they also care for school-age children. If, for example, you have a particularly demanding baby who perhaps cries a lot and is difficult to settle you may be very reluctant to take on the care of a boisterous three year-old or a fifteen month-old who is just beginning to walk.

Think very carefully before signing contracts and agreeing to care for extra children if you are already struggling with the children you are currently caring for. It is better to have places available to fill at a later stage, when you feel more confident, than to fill all your places immediately and struggle to provide good quality care.

Of course available places mean potential income and let us not forget that childminding is a job. However, always remember the importance of providing for the children to the best of your ability and, if you have little experience in caring for young children and are new to child-minding, you would be well advised to start off slowly and build your business up over an appropriate period of time.

TIP

When first setting up your business, pace yourself with regard to accepting new children. Start off slowly and build your business up at a rate which is easy for you to manage. Even if business is booming and you are inundated with enquiries, think carefully before agreeing to take on children of mixed ages and abilities.

A child's profile

It is a good idea to take the time to study the children you are caring for and, if necessary, create a 'profile' for each child. This is particularly helpful if you have places available but are unsure of whether or not you wish to fill them.

To help you to ascertain whether you will have the time and energy to devote to children of different ages, think about:

- the age of the children you are currently caring for;
- the stages of development of the children you are currently caring for;
- the potential for these stages to change over the next few months.

Registered childminders can usually care for:

> Six children under the age of eight years; of these, not more than three may be under five years, and of these, not more than one may be under one year at any one time. *National Standards for Under Eights Day Care and Childminding*, Ofsted.

If you are currently caring for a baby who is coming up to their first birthday and still have a place available for under fives, think carefully before agreeing to take on another child under one. You should take into account:

♦ The nature of the baby you are currently caring for. Are they clingy and demanding?

♦ What stage of development are they currently at? Are they crawling or walking?

♦ Will the child be crawling or walking in the very near future? This stage of a child's development is fraught with potential hazards, and whilst finding their feet, young children need you to be extra vigilant to prevent accidents.

♦ How would another young baby fit into your existing routine? Do you take or collect children from school? Will you need a double buggy, extra highchair or car seat?

Although all of these 'problems' can be solved think carefully about your own ability to cope with three young children. Be honest with yourself and look at all the aspects. There is nothing wrong with admitting that you can only cope with two children under the age of five and you will be a much better childminder for putting the child's welfare before your own interests.

9

Observations and Assessments

As you carry out your childminding duties, you will be observing and assessing the children in your care on a daily basis, probably without even realising you are doing it. Childminders have the advantage of working closely with the children in their care for lengthy periods of time, and will be in a position to get to know them well and watch them in an objective way to see exactly what they are doing and how they are behaving.

It is absolutely paramount that childminders spend some of their time carrying out observations and assessments of the children they are caring for in order to understand and meet their needs.

To be able to observe and assess children effectively you will need to learn how to watch them objectively and record your findings accurately. It is important to avoid making assumptions and judgements.

WHY DO CHILDMINDERS NEED TO OBSERVE THE CHILDREN IN THEIR CARE?

Observations and assessments are vital to a childminder's work for many different reasons. Effective observations and assessments enable the childminder to:

◆ understand the basic needs of the children in their care;

◆ ascertain which areas a particular child may need help and encouragement in;

◆ identify which areas of development a child is particularly good at;

◆ understand why a child acts in the way that they do, and to understand what provokes a certain kind of behaviour;

♦ share important developmental information with the child's parents, carers or other professionals;

♦ plan effective activities, suitable for the age and development of the children in their care;

♦ see whether a child is ill or showing signs of coming down with an illness;

♦ be alert to any obvious changes in a child's usual behaviour, which could indicate issues such as bullying, abuse, etc.

♦ be aware of any potential hazards around their home or garden and may highlight other dangers which may have been overlooked, for example, whilst on the school run or outings.

As a childminder you will get to know the children in your care very well. Over the weeks, months and years you will learn each child's special traits, their likes, dislikes, fears and anxieties. You will become a valued and trusted person in their lives and as such you will have the responsibility which comes with this very important role. Unlike in a nursery, where several carers may be responsible for different aspects of each child's care, you will have the sole responsibility of caring for the children registered with you and it is very important that you learn how to observe and assess their behaviour and development during the time they are with you and just as importantly, that you incorporate your findings during your day-to-day activities. There is little point in observing and assessing the children in your care if you are simply going to file away your recorded findings and not share the information with the child's parents or use it to plan your own activities and routines.

DEFINING 'OBSERVATION' AND 'ASSESSMENT'

Before we can fully understand how to carry out an observation or an assessment we must first know what each term really means.

Observation

Observation involves the gathering of information about a particular child's behaviour and their stage of development.

You will need to seek parental approval before carrying out an observation of a child. When seeking approval, inform the parents of the following:

1. Why you feel an observation would be beneficial.
2. What you are hoping your observation will achieve or reveal.
3. How you feel the observation will assist you in planning for the child's future needs.

You will also need to reassure the parents that you will share the information from the observation with them, and that all the details will remain confidential and will be accessed only by them, yourself and any other professionals on a 'need to know basis'. Always point out to the parents that the reason for an observation is to focus on the *positive* aspects of the child's behaviour and progress rather than looking to produce a *negative* list of underachievement.

Assessment

Assessment is your own unbiased, objective reflection on the information you have gathered during your observation.

Before finalising your assessment, you should discuss your observational findings with the child's parents, and if necessary any other professionals, in order for them to add their own comments, opinions and ideas. The results of your assessment should form an essential part of your future planning and they should be used to monitor the child's progress.

Now that we have accurately defined both observations and assessments we will look closely at the ways in which these essential childminding duties can be carried out effectively.

METHODS FOR OBSERVING AND ASSESSING CHILDREN

The main methods for observing children are as follows:

◆ event sampling;
◆ time sampling;
◆ target child;
◆ diaries;
◆ flow charts;
◆ interval recording;
◆ participative;
◆ non-participative;
◆ duration recording;
◆ written;
◆ checklists and tick charts.

Let us look at these methods in more detail.

Event sampling

This method of observation is particularly helpful if there is an aspect of the child's behaviour that you or the child's parents are especially keen to change, for example thumb sucking, resorting to tantrums, and so on. Event sampling enables the childminder to record when the 'event' occurs and to make a note of the actual events leading up to it. Event sampling may need to be carried out over quite a long period of time in order to discover what triggers the behaviour before a strategy can be sought to change it.

Time sampling

This method of observation is similar to event sampling in that you are recording what the child is actually doing, however you will be making notes of the child's behaviour at fixed times and intervals throughout the day. You will need to decide exactly what aspect of the child's behaviour you are intending to focus on and then decide on a suitable time interval. This could be every 15 minutes for two hours, every 30 minutes throughout the morning, or for two minutes every half hour.

Target child

Childminders may find this particular observation method difficult to carry out unless they are only caring for one child, as it requires focusing on just the one child for quite a lengthy period of time which is not always possible with other children present. If you work with another childminder or an assistant you may find this method of observation easier to use. Target child observations are used more successfully in nurseries, playgroups and reception classes where children are usually in larger groups. Using codes to abbreviate certain words, such as 'A' for adult, 'TC' for target child, will enable you to record quickly your observations as you are witnessing the situation.

Diaries

These are an informal way of recording developmental changes such as sleep and feeding patterns in young babies and they can also be used to record favourite activities.

Flow charts

It has to be said that not all professional childminders are adept or enjoy lots of writing and, although a necessary part of the job, observations and assessments can be quite daunting to some of even the most experienced of childminders. By using flow charts you can eliminate the need for pages and pages of writing but still ensure that effective observations are being carried out. Flow charts are diagrams which show the activities and the equipment's layout. Lines can be drawn on the chart to show the activities the children take part in and different colours can be used to denote the age and sex of the child and the activities preferred.

Interval recording

This method of observation is similar to time sampling except you decide on a specific detail of a child's behaviour which you wish to observe and then watch the child over a short period of time.

Participative

This type of observation can sometimes be awkward to carry out as you will need to be involved in the chosen activity yourself, making it impossible to write down your findings whilst carrying out the observation. You will need to rely heavily on your memory, particularly if you do not get the chance to record your findings immediately after the activity is over. Participative observations, however, can still be very effective as children will often become more involved if an adult participates in an activity such as reading a story, building with bricks or dressing-up.

Non-participative

As the name suggests, with this type of observation the childminder does not become involved in the activity at all and remains as unobtrusive as possible. Their only role is to record what they are seeing.

Duration recording

Many parents, and indeed childminders, have been heard to moan about the length of time a particular activity has taken to set up and how little time it then holds a child's interest. It can be discouraging for a childminder who has spent the best part of two hours inflating a bouncy castle on the lawn only to see the children tire of it after bouncing for ten minutes! The secret to planning activities for the children in your care is to concentrate on what *they* enjoy doing and to focus on *their* preferences rather than your own. You may love baking and enjoy trying out new complicated recipes, for example, but you would be well advised to save the soufflés for when the children have gone home and concentrate on fairy cakes whilst baking with the four year-olds.

In order to understand what the children in your care actually enjoy doing, try using duration recording to plot how long a child spends on a particular activity. This method of observation can also be used to see how long a particular type of behaviour lasts, for example a tantrum.

Written

This is perhaps the most time consuming of all the methods of observation as it involves recording information about a child's growth and development or behaviour over a particular period of time. Written records give as much detailed information as possible of exactly what the child is doing over the period of time the observation is taking place. A written observation should not contain any assumptions and should be an objective view of what is actually happening. At the end of the written observation you may like to note any areas of concern and how you intend to progress using your findings.

Checklists and tick charts

Another relatively easy way of recording a child's progress without the need for lengthy written reports, is the use of checklists and tick charts. Once you have devised a suitable list or chart all you will need to do is to review periodically the progress of the child and record your findings. A tick chart may look something like this:

TICK CHART

Name of child

Age of child

Date

Activity	✓ Or ✗
Able to hold a paintbrush	
Able to hold a pencil	
Able to use scissors to cut paper	
Able to tie a shoe lace	
Able to fasten a button	
Able to catch a ball	
Able to throw a ball	
Able to kick a ball	
Able to ride a bicycle	

Obviously the statements you insert in your own tick chart will depend on the age of the child you are observing. For example, if you are using this method to observe a nine month-old baby the statements may read something like:

- Able to sit up unaided
- Able to pull themselves to a standing position
- Able to roll from front to back
- Able to roll from back to front
- Able to clap hands
- Able to wave goodbye
- Able to crawl, etc.

TYPES OF OBSERVATION

We have looked at *methods* of observations. Now let us take a look at the *types* of observation which are:

- naturalistic;
- structured;
- longitudinal;
- snapshot.

Naturalistic

These are so called because they are observations of children which are carried out in the child's usual surroundings. The observation allows the child to carry out tasks which they would normally carry out without any structuring being attempted by you, the observer.

Structured

This type of observation is the opposite of naturalistic in that the childminder has specifically set up a particular activity in order to observe how a child carries out a specific task. For example, an obstacle course could be created to observe a child's balance and co-ordination, or a painting activity to observe a child's fine motor skills.

Longitudinal

When you have settled into a pattern of regularly observing the children in your care and recording your findings you will begin to build up *longitudinal* records of observation, as your findings will show how the children in your care change and progress over a lengthy period of time. Each child's set of records and observations will be their *longitudinal* record which will enable the important adults in their lives, namely you, their childminder, and their parents, to identify the important milestones and achievements in their lives.

Snapshot

As the name suggests, this type of observation involves trying to achieve a 'snapshot' of how a child is behaving at any given period of time. For example, a snapshot observation of how a child reacts immediately after their parent has dropped them off may be helpful in trying to deal with a child who is clingy and difficult to settle.

Essential information to include

With all observations there is a certain amount of essential information which must be included such as:

* the child's name;
* the child's age;
* the date the observation was carried out;
* the activity the child was involved in during the observation;
* the number, ages and gender of any other children involved in the activity;
* the name of the person carrying out the observation.

When observing a child, use whichever method you are most comfortable with and whichever is appropriate for the purpose you wish to achieve. It is vital that the observation is accurate and unbiased. Refrain from taking away findings which you feel may upset or worry parents, as these may be vital clues to the overall assessment of the child.

For example, if you are observing a child's behaviour in order to develop an appropriate strategy to deal with tantrums, and simply to avoid embarrassing the child's parents you omit the fact that, during an observation, the child lashed out or threw a toy across the room, then you risk jeopardising the whole exercise as this is an important part of the child's behaviour which needs to be addressed.

Never exaggerate the situation or problem to make it appear worse than it really is. Your observations must be accurate and up to date to have any benefit whatsoever on the child's overall development.

TIP

Observations do not have to be lengthy, complicated accounts. Choose the method of observation you are most comfortable with and remember to record your findings *accurately.*

USING OBSERVATIONS TO PLAN FOR CHILDREN'S NEEDS

You will be making plans all the time without even realising you are doing so. Everyone makes plans at some time in their lives. They may be as simple as writing a shopping list or organising a trip to the park, or as complex as planning a special holiday or a wedding. Every day of our lives will involve some type of planning. If you have children of your own you will plan their day as well as your own. Planning will include what clothes to wear, food to buy and cook, activities to enjoy, places to go, etc. Most of the planning we do on a daily basis will be done in our heads with the occasional written reminder to jog our memories of important things lest we forget.

Planning is an important part of a childminder's day. In order for the day to run smoothly and for everything to get done on time, plans need to be made *and* implemented. Plans are vital for the effective and efficient running of a childminding business. Childminders should be making plans on both a daily and a weekly basis, and depending on the number and ages of children in their care, the plans may look something like this:

DAILY CHILDMINDING PLAN

Important times to adhere to:

1. Arrival of children from   7.30am onwards
2. Drop off at school   8.50am
3. Drop off at playgroup   9.00am
4. Collect from playgroup   11.30am
5. Lunch time   12 noon
6. Collect from school   3.30pm
7. Tea   4.30pm
8. Departure of children from   5.00pm onwards

With the exception of the above times, the rest of the childminder's day can be planned to their own agenda, doing activities to suit the children's preferences and the opportunities which arise. It is essential that the times above are adhered to and that the children are taken to and collected from school and playgroup on time. Meals must be planned at regular times everyday to avoid the children becoming overly hungry or having to rush meals in order to fit them in. If children usually leave your house by 5pm you must make sure that they have been fed and are ready to be collected as agreed. Parents will not be impressed if, after a hard day at work, they then have to wait half an hour for their child to eat their tea because you failed to time your own day effectively.

TIP

Never plan your day so stringently that there is no room for manoeuvre. Always allow sufficient time for spontaneous play and allow children to enjoy activities at their own pace rather than having to stick to a rigid time schedule.

By sticking to a workable plan you should be able to carry out your childminding duties satisfactorily and progress onto effective weekly planning which may incorporate things like:

◆ visiting the library;

- shopping for essentials for your childminding business;
- specific homework on set days for school children;
- outings;
- activities for the week.

TIP

It is important to remember that there is no right or wrong way to plan. How you plan your working day and week is entirely up to you. What is important, however, is that the plans you make meet your own needs and those of the children you care for.

The observations you have carried out will put you in good stead when deciding on how to plan for the needs of the children in your care. For example your observations and assessments will enable you to:

- see which activities the children enjoy the most;
- see which activities the children are least interested in;
- determine which activities a child is good at;
- decide how to extend the activity in order to stretch the skills of the child;
- check the child's progress and growth.

When to extend activities

The more information you can have about a child in your care the better equipped you should be to provide for their needs. Always take your cue from the child and never try to over stretch them before they are ready. When you have found an activity which the child enjoys, introduce it as often as they wish but refrain from extending it until they are competent enough to cope with more complexity. If you try to push a child too far too soon you risk alienating them and their self-confidence may even suffer if they feel they have failed in a particular task.

A child of two who has just discovered the joy of painting, for example, by using a variety of finger paints, paint pads and sponges should be allowed to experiment in this way before you introduce more complex materials such as brushes, scrapers, stamps, string, etc. Avoid the temptation to indulge them with too many varied and complex materials before they are ready and always be realistic with your expectations.

Likewise, there is little point in planning an activity involving making a collage with a child who cannot yet use scissors correctly. Instead allow the child the time to practise using scissors on a regular basis and then, when they are confident with this task, introduce making a simple collage.

> **TIP**
>
> Remember, activities should offer the child a 'happy medium' without being too easy or too difficult.

EVALUATIONS

Planning, observing and assessing children are all very important aspects of a childminder's duties, however without evaluation all of the other tasks will have been a waste of time.

Evaluation is the method of judging how much progress the child has actually made over a period of time. Evaluations need to be continuous and systematic, and they need to take into account the child's past experiences.

Children are changing all the time and this is why evaluations need to be carried out. As the children grow and progress, you will need to alter your routines and activities to take into account these changes. Childminders will benefit from evaluating not only the children in their care and the activities they provide, but also the materials and resources they have on offer and the space and time available.

Evaluations will enable you to:

◆ encourage the children to concentrate on certain areas of their development;

- ◆ encourage the children to develop an interest in a variety of areas and activities;

- ◆ ascertain whether the children are playing well together and if there are any areas of behaviour which are causing you concern;

- ◆ decide whether the toys and equipment available are appropriate for the children's ages and stages of development and what new toys and equipment may be beneficial;

- ◆ decide whether any new learning materials will benefit the children;

- ◆ ascertain whether the activities already enjoyed are stretching the children's ability and imagination appropriately and whether these need to be assessed.

Figure 10 shows the continuous cycle of observing and assessing children in your care, evaluating the results of your own childminding practice, implementing any changes you feel are necessary and planning the future care of the children together with appropriate activities.

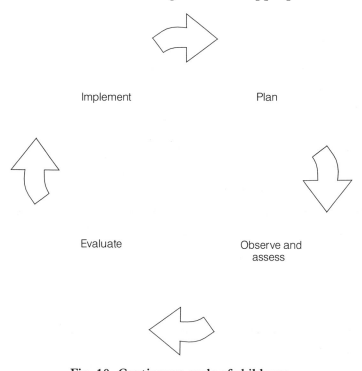

Implement   Plan

Evaluate   Observe and
                          assess

Fig. 10. Continuous cycle of childcare.

Respecting each child's individuality

By observing, assessing and evaluating the children in your care you will be able to build up an accurate picture of each child, based on their individuality and preferences. Any preconceived ideas of what you personally *expect* from each child must be forgotten and you should aim at all times to avoid speculation or allowing yourself to be influenced by prior knowledge. Avoid making comparisons and remember that all children are individuals, unique in every aspect of their make-up and should be treated with understanding, love and respect.

TIP

You may be very surprised by what you learn from your observations and assessments and any preconceived ideas must be forgotten. It is, for example, perfectly natural for a girl to enjoy kicking a football around and taking part in rough and tumble games which are so often associated as being primarily 'boys' games'. Equally, there is nothing wrong with a boy who enjoys taking part in dressing-up, baking and playing with dolls. Allow the children to find their own preferences and avoid conveying stereotypical ideas at all times.

Discussing certain evaluations with parents

When evaluating your observations and assessments there may be times when it is apparent to you that something is amiss and that a certain course of action may be necessary. For example, your observations may have revealed a medical problem which may need referral. Always discuss your findings and worries with the child's parents and decide, together, what course of action should be taken. Be sensitive to the parents' feelings if you suspect their child has some kind of medical problem and take the time to offer support and reassurance. Often something like a hearing impairment is short lived and may be the result of a particularly heavy cold; however more severe problems will need ongoing treatment and the parents may feel very vulnerable at this time.

SELF-EVALUATION

The importance of self-evaluation

You can never know too much about childcare no matter how experienced a childminder you may be. A childminder who feels that they have no room for improvement and need not continue with updating their own professional training and skills is, to my mind, a poor childminder. Childcare practice is an ever changing profession and it is absolutely essential that you keep up to date with practice and procedures.

No business, whether it be a childminding business or not, will develop if the people running it are unwilling or unable to move forward. You should always be looking for ways to make your childminding business better and to increase your own skills and knowledge. Like the children we are caring for, we are learning new things and gaining new skills every day.

Although it is probably true to say that no one enjoys being criticised, try not to look on all criticism as being negative. Sometimes criticism, given in the right way, can be extremely beneficial and can help us to see things from a different perspective.

TIP
Constructive criticism should be welcomed, valued and acted upon.

In order for you to be a reflective practitioner it is necessary for you to systematically evaluate yourself and the way in which you carry out your childminding duties. Just because you have been doing things in a set way for several years and they *appear* to be working well does not mean that this is the most effective way you could be working. By using self-evaluation methods you will be able to evaluate your own childminding practice and reflect upon your own skills to decide how effective your system actually is.

How to evaluate your childminding practice

Try asking yourself the following questions:

1. Is there anything I can do to improve the service I provide?
2. Is there anything I can do to improve the qualifications I have?
3. What areas of my childminding skills do I need to improve upon?
4. Is my business running effectively?
5. Are the children in my care happy and content?
6. Are the children in my care achieving the goals I have set for them?
7. Are the children in my care reaching the developmental 'norms'?

Possible areas for additional training

It is not always easy to carry out a self-assessment objectively. However by looking at each aspect of your childminding business you should be able to ascertain which areas you need additional training in. If, for example, you are caring for a child with a particular disability, you should be seeking additional training to help you carry out your duties effectively. Likewise, if you have not undertaken any training in Birth to Three Matters and you are caring for a baby you should consider enrolling on an appropriate course.

Child protection issues are also 'grey' areas for many childminders who may have only briefly looked at these issues whilst on other courses. All childminders should be competent in child protection issues and know how to spot signs of abuse and how to report them.

First aid is another aspect of a childminder's training which needs to be regularly updated.

Parents' ideas and suggestions

Consider asking the parents of the children you are caring for to complete a simple questionnaire which you have devised. The questionnaire should ask the parents to comment on areas of your childcare practice such as the menus and activities you provide, how happy they consider their children to be. It is always a good idea to 'invite' parents to add their own ideas or to suggest areas for improvement.

Don't look at the results of the questionnaires as criticism but use the parents' comments to improve the service you provide. You may find that parents, who often wouldn't say anything to you face to face, have a lot to say when invited to give their comments on a questionnaire!

Of course if you are going to offer parents the chance to tell you truthfully what they think, you must be prepared to take their comments on board and make any necessary changes to your routines. If a parent requests something specifically which you are unable to carry out, explain why it is not possible for you to do it, and try to offer a compromise. Never ignore a suggestion made by a parent, as they may feel as if their opinions are unimportant and that is the very last thing you should be striving to achieve. Always remember that happy parents are just as important to your childminding business as happy children!

Useful Addresses and Websites

British Red Cross
9 Grosvenor Square
London
SW1X 7EJ
Telephone: 020 7235 5454
Website: www.redcross.org.uk
Email: info@redcross.org.uk

ChildLine
Freepost 1111
London
W1 0BR
Telephone: 0800 1111
Website: www.childline.org.uk

Children's Play Council
8 Wakely Street
London
EC1V 7QE
Telephone: 020 7843 6016
Website: www.ncb.org.uk/cpc

End Physical Punishment of Children (EPOCH)
77 Holloway Road
London
N7 8JZ
Telephone: 020 7700 0627
Website: www.epoch-worldwide@mcr1.poptel.org.uk

Equal Opportunities Commission
Arndale House
Arndale Centre
Manchester
M4 3EQ
Telephone: 0845 601 5901
Website: www.eoc.org.uk
Email: info@eoc.org.uk

Hyperactive Children's Support Group
71 Whyke Lane
Chichester
PO19 7PD
Telephone: 01243 551313
Website: www.hacsg.org.uk
Email: contact@hacsg.org.uk

National Association for Toy and Leisure Libraries
68 Churchway
London
NW1 1LT
Telephone: 020 7387 9592
Website: www.natll.org.ukadmin@natll.ukf.net

National Council for One Parent Families
255 Kentish Town Road
London
NW5 2LX
Telephone: 020 7428 5400
Website: www.oneparentfamilies.org.uk
Email: info@oneparentfamilies.org.uk

National Society for the Prevention of Cruelty to Children (NSPCC)
National Centre
42 Curtain Road
London
EC2A 3NH

Telephone: 020 7825 2500 or
Helpline: 0808 800 5000
Website: www.nspcc.org.uk

Pre-School Learning Alliance
69 Kings Cross Road
London
WC1X 9LL
Telephone: 020 7833 0991
Website: www.pre-school.org.uk
Email: pla@pre-school.org.uk

Royal Society for the Prevention of Accidents (RoSPA)
Edgbaston Park
353 Bristol Road
Edgbaston
Birmingham
B5 7ST
Telephone: 0121 248 2000
Website: www.rospa.com
Email: help@rospa.co.uk

Kidscape
www.kidscape.org.uk

WEBSITES FOR CHILDREN

CBBC Newsround Online www.bbc.co.uk/newsround
Cybertales www.cybertales.co.uk
The Big Bus www.thebigbus.com
Juniorszone www.juniorszone.com

Further Reading

Bruce, T. (2001) *Learning Through Play: Babies, Toddlers and the Foundation Years,* London: Hodder & Stoughton.

Hobart, C. and Frankel, J. (1999) *A Practical Guide to Activities for Young Children,* Cheltenham: Nelson Thornes.

Leach, P. (2003) *Your Baby and Child,* Oxford: Dorling Kindersley.

Lee, A. (2006) *Starting Your Own Childminding Business,* Oxford: How to Books.

Meggitt, C. (1999) *Caring for Babies,* London: Hodder & Stoughton.

Index